D0915238

WITHDRAWN FROM
MACALESTER COLLEGE
LIBRARY

THE CONCEPTION OF VALUE

The Conception of Value

PAUL GRICE

With an Introduction by
JUDITH BAKER

CLARENDON PRESS · OXFORD
1991

Oxford University Press, Walton Street, Oxford OX2 6DP
Oxford New York Toronto
Delhi Bombay Calcutta Madras Karachi
Petaling Jaya Singapore Hong Kong Tokyo
Nairobi Dar es Salaam Cape Town
Melbourne Auckland
and associated companies in
Berlin Ibadan

Oxford is a trade mark of Oxford University Press

Published in the United States
by Oxford University Press, New York

© Kathleen Grice 1991

All rights reserved. No part of this publication may be reproduced,
stored in a retrieval system, or transmitted, in any form or by any means,
electronic, mechanical, photocopying, recording, or otherwise, without
the prior permission of Oxford University Press

This book is sold subject to the condition that it shall not, by way
of trade or otherwise, be lent, re-sold, hired out or otherwise circulated
without the publisher's prior consent in any form of binding or cover
other than that in which it is published and without a similar condition
including this condition being imposed on the subsequent purchaser

British Library Cataloguing in Publication Data
data available

Library of Congress Cataloging in Publication Data
Grice, H. P. (H. Paul)
The conception of value/Paul Grice: with an introduction by
Judith Baker.
Includes bibliographical references and index.
1. Values. I. Title.
B1641.G481 1991 121'.8—dc20 90–26891
ISBN 0–19–824495–9

Typeset by Cambrian Typesetters
Frimley, Camberley, Surrey
Printed in Great Britain by
Biddles Ltd.
Guildford & King's Lynn

Foreword

Paul Grice wrote and delivered his Carus lectures on the conception of value in 1983. He returned to the topic of those lectures, and in particular to the construction of value, in the course of responding to essays written in his honour. Shortly before he died, he asked me to publish the lectures, but with the argument for value sketched in his 'Reply' replacing the one presented in the third and final lecture. He regarded his later attempt as a clarification, better representing his thought. Unfortunately no straightforward substitution is possible. It seemed better to allow the reader direct access to the work of Paul Grice, and so his Carus lectures are published below in their entirety, followed by the relevant section of the 'Reply'. Since he and I had discussed the problems over the preceding decade, my Introduction describes one way to understand the most difficult of Grice's new ideas about value, and the relationship between the third lecture and the 'Reply'.

The lectures themselves were edited by comparing the manuscript (to be deposited in the Paul Grice Archives, University of California at Berkeley) and a rough typescript version he had made in 1983. Aside from minor typographical emendations, the two previously published essays—the Reply and an address to the American Philosophical Association—are unaltered.

In the footnotes, editorial notes and insertions are indicated by enclosure in square brackets.

J. B.

Contents

Introduction

Judith Baker

H. P. GRICE'S CONSTRUCTION OF VALUE

The three works of Paul Grice collected in this volume were selected in order to present his metaphysical defence of value. The Carus lectures and the selection from the 'Reply to Richards' take value as their topic. The APA address, 'Method in Philosophical Psychology (from the Banal to the Bizarre)', an essay in philosophical psychology, is included for its exposition of Humean Projection, a metaphysical 'routine' Grice made the basis for the construction of value. This introduction will attempt to clarify some of the basic elements of Grice's constructivist theory and the relationship between the third Carus lecture and the 'Reply'.

In 1983 Paul Grice gave the Carus lectures, the Conception of Value. The lectures, particularly the third and last, on the metaphysical construction of value, were difficult to understand. He returned to the topic in his reply to essays written in his honour. Although the later account was meant to clarify and improve the earlier argument, the lectures remain difficult. The one on the construction of value is an essay in metaphysics and not on or within ethics or theory of value. It is indeed not clear how those theories get attached to the work. One difficulty is that both the Carus lecture and the 'Reply' call on a number of philosophical themes which interested Grice for a long time, but which were not among the more widely publicized aspects of his work. What is referred to in the

Carus lectures as Humean Projection explained the growth of conceptualization and representation in progressively more complex creatures. It was part of an enterprise in creature-construction, first introduced in the Urbana lectures of 1970–1 on 'Language and Reality' (unpublished). It was fully developed and played a large part in the APA address. Discussion of this address is limited here to the topic of Humean Projection, but it is an enormously rich essay. It attempted both to understand psychological concepts as theoretical concepts explaining behaviour and to account for the privileged position of some of those concepts. The third Carus lecture asserts, and its argument relies on, an interdependence of the notions of finality and value. Like the discussion of freedom, the discussion of finality occupied Grice for many years, but it was perhaps not fully accomplished. The importance of the philosophical attempt invites us, however, to work to understand the lectures.

For they are a modern effort to provide a metaphysical foundation for value. Value judgements are viewed as objective, value is part of the world we live in, none the less value is constructed by us. Grice's story puts together a number of seemingly divergent elements and attempts to make them work together. We inherit, or seem to inherit, the Aristotelian world in which objects and creatures are characterized, perceived, understood in terms of finality features, namely, what they are supposed to do. We are thereby enabled to evaluate by reference to, or relative to, function and finality. That is not surprising. However, Grice maintains that the legitimacy of such evaluations rests ultimately on an argument for absolute value. Grice thinks that vitalistic phenomena can be explained by mechanistic, cybernetic notions, but he insists that explanations in terms of finality and attributions of relative value are none the less both legitimate and irreducible. This claim depends on the thesis that the reducibility and substitutability of finality features may be blocked in all areas if there is one area in which attribution of finality has no substitute. The non-substitutable attribution of finality accompanies absolute value and so must rest on Grice's argument for absolute value. Value is itself overtly constructed, but not from such naturalistic items as desires or desires to desire. Our attitudes, which provide the basis for value, are irreducible modes of "thinking-valuable" or "feeling-valuable". (But you must hear the hyphens between the terms, which indicate that we do not have at the start an object or the representation of an object.)

This introduction will take as its focus what Grice calls construction routines. They are essential to the argument for the construction of objective value. The attempt to understand them raises very general questions about Grice's conception of transcendental arguments and objectivity. In what follows, the metaphysical operations are interpreted in the light of the prototypical Humean Projection, not as invented procedures but as natural dispositions to take the world to be a certain way. So interpreted, they can be seen to carry certain of the features of the objectivity sought: *consensus* via commonality of conception, and also *non-arbitrariness*, for the conceptualization does not depend upon individual will or whim. Routines answer a criticism of the alleged objectivity of constructed value: they remove a threatened gap between the justified acceptance of a construction thesis and legitimate belief in its truth.

It may help to understand the role of the routines in Grice's theory of value to have an outline, a sketch of the formal structure of the third Carus lecture. I include a list of the main elements, although one cannot expect to find the steps in the argument immediately understandable from such a display. It is offered as a reference, to which one can return. I have made use of material from the 'Reply' where it helps to clarify the argument. In particular, *value of a kind* is introduced in the 'Reply' as an important step in the defence of absolute value. Although the steps are not easy to understand, the project can be simply stated: Grice's goal is to show that some value judgements are objective, and to do this by displaying their construction. Two routines are involved in the construction: one, Humean Projection, accounts for the projection of attitudes onto the world, the other, provocatively called Metaphysical Transubstantiation, for a new kind of creature or substance. They work together for the legitimacy of projection, as constructing value or placing value in the world depends upon the status of the projector.

According to Grice, a value judgement—one that is objective—has the following construction history:

1. Such a judgement starts off life as a human attitude, a mode of "thinking-valuable".

2. Hume attributed to the mind a tendency 'to spread itself upon objects', to project into the world items which properly or primitively considered are only features of our states of mind.[1] Grice delighted in the description, but he wanted to reverse Hume's implication. What Hume diagnosed as a source of illusion and confusion becomes, under specified conditions, a legitimate construction procedure. Grice's Humean Projection occurs by stages: intermediate stages reflect a growing logical complexity, the new concept is embedded within a more general psychological attitude, then within another embeddable

---

[1] ' 'Tis a common observation, that the mind has a great propensity to spread itself on external objects, and to conjoin with them any internal impressions, which they occasion, and which always make their appearance at the same time that these objects discover themselves to the senses' (*Treatise*, I. iii. xliv).

Later, writing of reason and taste, Hume said that 'The one discovers objects as they really stand in nature, without addition or diminution; the other has a productive faculty, and gilding or staining all natural objects with the colours, borrowed from internal sentiment, raises in a manner a new creation' (*Enquiry*, Appendix 1). This text has also captured the attention of Simon Blackburn, *Spreading the Word* (Oxford: Oxford University Press, 1984), 145.

operator. At the final stage, what characterized thinking characterizes the object of thinking. "Thinking-valuable" becomes judging something to be of value. The legitimacy of this move depends on two conditions: that there is a rational demand for the new concept of value (indeed, that there is a rational demand for each new stage) and that at the final stage there are 'truth conditions, or something analogous' for the judgements in which value occurs.

3. The rational demand for absolute value is not fully argued for. This legitimating condition is variously described as *a theoretical* motivation or purpose in the Carus lectures, and *a rational* demand in the 'Reply'. In the latter work, Grice refers to what is most likely a transcendental or, his preferred term, metaphysical argument as the supporting consideration.

4. Grice provides not truth conditions but something analogous for statements of value. He answers to the demand for absolute value by telling a 'trouble-free' or good story of how we might construct it. The legitimacy of substituting a convincing story for truth conditions is derived from a principle Grice dubs the metaphysical principle of supply and demand; he meant this title, entertaining as it is, with high seriousness. It is a principle, he said, 'which allows credence to a set of procedures the adoption and use of which will most satisfactorily meet a rational need'.

5. The story begins:

(*a*) by characterizing living creatures, including humans, essentially, in terms of finality features. What the creatures *are* is understood in terms of what they *do*; certain of their states and behaviour are such that the creature aspires to them, sets out to do them (and, in the case of humans, consciously so).

(*b*) Finality or function provides us with a standard for evaluating both behaviour and creatures. A theory of conduct, or of behaviour, can be generated from the starting-point of function; and a creature that does what it is supposed to do is good *qua* that kind of creature. Grice claims, explicitly in the 'Reply', implicity in the third Carus lecture, that relative value judgements depend upon finality; we can legitimately evaluate creatures, given finality features and the derivable theory of behaviour.[2]

(*c*) A human being has as an *accidental* property a complex attribute called rationality, defined as (at least partly) the capacity and concern that its attitudes be well-grounded, or validated. A thoroughgoing concern to have reasons brings with it a concern to find some attitudes, decisions, beliefs, absolutely validated (or of absolute value).

(*d*) This accidental property becomes the *essential* property of, and thereby provides for, a new kind of creature, *persons*. Human beings redistribute their properties, 'reconstitute' themselves as persons, as essentially rational, via a routine called Metaphysical Transubstantiation.

(*e*) We can then characterize a person who is good at her function or *métier* of finding reasons, as good *qua* person.

(*f*) It is characteristic of humans and persons to

---

[2] Relative value judgements depend upon finality, but finality must be a genuine, 'non-Pickwickian' concept. Grice devotes half of the third Carus lecture to the question of the substitutability of finality by cybernetic or mechanistic notions. I cannot discuss this large question in this paper, but the form of his argument is the following: vitalistic phenomena form a domain in which both explanations in terms of finality and cybernetic notions are acceptable. If, however, there is an area in which cybernetic or mechanistic explanations cannot do the work of finality, we may regard finality as non-substitutable in *all* areas. He proceeds to argue that the characterization of person in terms of finality features provides for such an area. And that this is because persons, as essentially rational beings, are free. I conjecture that "free" does the following work: the behaviour of persons who seek ultimate justifications goes beyond what is biologically useful; the principles or procedures for answering their demand to find ultimate reasons must be constructed by them; a rewrite in mechanistic terms thus seems to be precluded.

'project' their 'thinking-valuable'; they judge and speak of the objects of their thinking as valuable. But the move is legitimated in the case of a *person* good at her *métier*; her value is transmitted to what she "thinks-valuable".

(g) The transmitted value may be viewed as absolute. If the value of persons were relative, the value transmitted would be relative. But persons as good *qua* members of a kind may be viewed as candidates for primary examples of what is of absolute value. Grice argues for granting them that status on the basis of the metaphysical principle of supply and demand. The projection routine or procedure is a way by which we might extend the range of value judgements if we could start with persons being of absolute value. We could then get the absolute value we as rational beings legitimately demand.

The operation flauntingly named Metaphysical Transubstantiation is a procedure for the redistribution, but not the invention, of properties. What was accidental becomes essential. Rationality, which in Grice's account attaches only *accidentally* to *humans*, becomes via this construction routine an *essential* property of *persons*.[3] Although there is no new stuff in the world, the world is meant to be richer as a result of this metaphysical routine. If the title has had its full provocative effect, the reader needs some distance from what is supposed to happen to humans in their

---

[3] 'They [humans] do not alter the totality of attributes which each of them as humans possess, but they redistribute them; properties which they possess essentially as humans become properties which as substances of a new psychological type called *persons* they possess accidentally; and the property or properties called rationality, which attached only accidentally to humans, attaches essentially to persons. While each human is standardly coincident with a particular person (and is indeed, perhaps, identical with that person over a time), logic is insufficient to guarantee that there will not come a time when that human and that person are no longer identical, when *one* of them, perhaps, but not the other, has ceased to exist.' ('Reply to Richards', *Philosophical Grounds of Rationality: Intentions, Categories, Ends*, ed. Richard Grandy and Richard Warner (Oxford: Oxford University Press, 1986), 102; see p. 114 below.)

passage to personhood. More modest examples must illustrate how such a metaphysical construction works and with what justice we may think of this procedure, in general, as a natural disposition.

Here are some mundane examples of something like metaphysical transubstantiation, three candidates for new entities that come into being in that way. First, sheepdogs. Suppose that there are dogs which have the herding characteristic, that a dog which attached itself to a shepherd exhibited this feature, and that the shepherd came to exploit and develop what he found in this animal. The dog has as an *accidental* property a capacity and desire to herd. To conceive of this property as *essential* would be to think of an animal whose job or function it is to herd sheep, and this of course is what we mean by a sheepdog. But so far, although we have introduced an expression whose use is evident we could not, says Grice, claim that a new kind of entity had come into being. We would have only 'a new way of speaking'.

What more is needed, to move from new words to new entities? It is plausible to suppose that there is a tendency to reconceive things in terms of their usefulness to us, to shift the emphasis of the properties which characterize them. The new way of speaking arises from or is rather part of it. If there is such a natural disposition, or construction routine, at work, it creates a new kind of entity according to Grice only if there is legitimate and legitimating motivation; thus a theoretical purpose, which would be served if we could show that we can extend to the new entity needed explanations. The following motivations seem relevant to establish such a purpose: first, we would like to be able to extend to the dog those forms of explanation which involve attitudes toward work previously restricted to humans. We need to explain the sheepdog's behaviour using such notions as recognition of a task, eagerness to get to it, perception that help is needed. We may explain a particular old sheepdog's longevity as we do a person's, in terms of its desire to get its work done. The new kind of animal is one that essentially co-operates with a human in a job, that can indeed be said to have a job.

Second, we will want to justify treating our co-worker animals in a way different from the way in which we treat wild animals. That is, we may want to extend not only principles of explanation, but also practical principles.

It is not in itself the *use* we make of an animal with herding instincts which brings into being a new kind of entity, nor even the training which develops the animal's natural capacities. Although our use and training may bring into the world a particular example of the kind, the construction of the kind is distinct; it is possible only given the shift in concept coupled with a legitimate demand for an entity of the given type. There is an additional observation to be made here. The shift in conception in the case of sheepdogs may be what a purposive human requires in order to engage in the activities involving the animals. What can then be viewed as a necessary pre-supposition for engaging in those activities backs (or can be used to back) the claim that a new kind of entity has been constructed.

Reference to two additional examples will allow us to raise questions about the two kinds of motivation for the introduction of new entities. Pets and tools exemplify the redistribution of properties typical of Metaphysical Transubstantiation. However, the legitimating motivation seems purely practical. We would like to extend practical principles, possibly, in the case of pets, via an extension of the notion of legitimate expectations. A pet's expectations could then be understood to derive from the kinds of dependency we previously held ourselves responsible for only with respect to humans.

The first tools may have been coincident with found natural objects which exhibited features useful to humans. The practical need to conserve the most apt of these, to

keep other humans from casually disposing of them, and
to enjoy the advantages of trading for them and improving
them, provides practical motivation for the new kind of
entity, for the redistribution of properties, such that a tool
is *essentially* what is able to do certain work for us. Tools
are essentially valuable to us, and so whatever practical
principles apply to guarding, conserving, and caring for
what is valuable get extended to them.

It might be argued that there is no mystery (and hence
nothing metaphysically exciting) in our changing behaviour
and practices, in extending practical principles, in these
two examples. For all that is at issue is the way *we* treat the
object, not the object's behaviour. This is why purely
theoretical motivation (as in the sheepdog example) seems
to provide stronger support for a new entity. It is not clear
how much weight one should give this criticism: first, it is
only our conception and our subsequent behaviour which
is at issue in the case of those social constructions like
money which we accept as part of the world. Second,
where the constructed entities have their place in the world
of practice or action, the appropriate justification may well
exemplify what Grice thought to be one pattern of
transcendental arguments: some area of local rationality,
or as we might paraphrase, some forms of behaviour and
human activity would be unintelligible and unavailable to
us without the disputed entity. Grice himself shifts, as
noted, in calling first for theoretical motivation, and then
for a rational demand, in order to legitimize construction
of a new entity.

How are we to understand the application of this
routine in the case of persons? Although Grice does not
raise the question, if his argument is to go through, it must
be possible to see at work here a natural disposition to
conceive of the world (or of ourselves) in certain ways. His
claim is that there is a rational demand for absolute value
which can be satisfied by finding a being whose essence it
is to establish and to apply forms of absolute value, and

that such a being can be obtained by Metaphysical Transubstantiation. It is accompanied by a suggestion-for-an-argument to show that there is a rational demand for absolute value. Once the rational need or demand for such an entity has been established, Grice can invoke the 'Metaphysical Principle of Supply and Demand'. Certainly Grice meant to provide *justification*: for the construction routine of Metaphysical Transubstantiation and so for the entity constructed. The suggested argument for absolute value seems to be his answer to why humans would engage in this routine.

Although complicated by the fact that two constructions are involved—absolute value and persons—the general pattern is clear. We need absolute value, and persons can provide it. Although it is not likely that anyone is actually motivated to engage in the construction routine by such a thought, this does not show Grice's account to be faulty. His theory, which describes both the justifying principles and the forms of construction, may be seen as displaying our ability to construct without supposing the routines to be actual, historical, processes. It is an ability we must have to satisfy our rational demands. But the philosophical task of constructing value cannot be viewed as one of simply showing how it is possible for value to be constructed. For that there is absolute value is contested, and the philosopher needs to do more to establish that a new entity has been constructed.

It may be that the construction routines, understood as natural ways to conceive or reconceive the world, can do much to account for the objectivity of our construction. The rationale which Grice offers as justification for the routine of Metaphysical Transubstantiation, that it will get us absolute value, will need to be supplemented by an arguably natural tendency to redistribute the property of rationality. Plausible motivation must be found which can arguably be attributed to most or many, if not all, humans. For a human performs Metaphysical Transubstantiation

only on herself. And if Grice's metaphysical essay is to
provide a foundation for ethics, we clearly want it to be the
case that most, if not all, humans are persons and so of
absolute value.

The difficulty does not lie in finding *some* natural
disposition on our part to re-evaluate our own characteristics. No doubt individuals may fairly commonly shift
in their sense of what is central to who they are; but one
needs to find rationality the focus of such a change over a
common enough ground. Two examples seem likely
candidates for Grice's redistribution of properties. One's
integrity might be at issue in a given moral dilemma, and
provoke a reconception-cum-commitment on the part of
the agent to be a certain sort of person, namely, one for
whom ultimately justifiable principles for action and
thought are central. A given commitment to theoretical
endeavour might also be interpreted in this way. Certainly
moral behaviour and theoretical practice would provide
admirable examples of a common human activity in which
a demand for a new entity could arise. But what is needed
is a way to see how it is that the reconception prompted by
issues of integrity makes those activities intelligible and
possible.

A third candidate may be more helpful. It is important
to remember that Grice would not have regarded what is
called 'rational choice theory' as an adequate study of
rationality. He understood rationality to include a concern
for justified or validated attitudes and decisions, a concern
which questions the desirability or propriety of ends as
well as the means taken to achieve them. Humans possess
rationality as an accidental property. But Grice does not
say what difference it would make for this property of
rationality to be *essential*, apart from the attribution of
value which is made possible by the change. A speculation:
although humans look for justification, are motivated to
find reasons for their attitudes, even ultimate ones, we
cannot expect them to be fully thoroughgoing in their

search. Should the principles they propose for themselves or the search for them seriously conflict with self-interest, they will not withstand the challenge. Only an individual with an essential or central concern to have justified attitudes can reasonably be expected to withstand the conflicts posed by self-interest.

Here is a suggestion for the kind of redistribution of one's properties we are looking for. When we engage in a co-operative venture with other humans which is based on agreement, and where compliance contains elements of trust, our activity is intelligible only if we conceive of ourselves and the others as essentially rational. Although in the act of identifying myself with this kind of group I only construct one given individual instance, myself, I do this via construction of the type. An additional benefit of the example of trust is that, even if we suppose (for reasons not discussed) that a human must perform the routine of Metaphysical Transubstantiation on herself, the construction envisaged in trust requires conceiving of other humans as persons and so treating them as persons.

The underlying ideas here are familiar: insofar as I think of the general truth 'we are all alike, we all stand to gain by doing this together', I need impute nothing more than self-interest to myself and others. I can think our capacity to engage in, and act on the basis of, reason-giving to be essentially prompted by and limited by our self-interest. But if I believe myself and others to be the kind of creature concerned with standards of acceptability which are not inherently limited by the criterion of self-interest and preservation, if I think we are concerned to find acceptable rules of conduct which are maximally general and which can be justified to other rational beings, then I think of us as that new kind of species, persons.

I need not, of course, use the term "persons": insofar as my expectations that others will keep their part of the agreement extends beyond what could be expected on the basis of their calculation of self-interest, I exercise trust.

That others are essentially rational, concerned to justify their actions, would make that trust intelligible, as well as justifiable. There is good reason to suppose not only that we often trust others in this way, but that there is such a natural tendency or disposition on the part of human beings. For such a disposition is biologically useful; to get on with the business of life in a community some modicum of trust is essential. This is a good example for the thesis that the construction routines are best viewed not as invented procedures but as natural tendencies to take the world to be a certain way.

We may now turn to the issue of *Humean Projection*. Hume attributed to the mind a tendency 'to spread itself upon objects', to project into the world items which properly or primitively considered are only features of our states of mind. What served as a diagnosis of one source of illusion becomes, under specified conditions, a legitimizing procedure in Grice. It is important to remember that many instances of projecting our wishes and attitudes onto the world do not carry reason or objectivity with them. We find things and people bleak or hateful, awesome, ace, charming, and likeable; we use the vocabulary of our passions to describe the world, but this does not by itself alter what there is.

Grice thought of Hume's description of the mind's disposition to project as prototypical of the procedure he envisaged. He described two important applications of Humean Projection. Their differences arise mainly from the purposes for which Grice deployed them. In the APA address he wished to legitimize the attribution to creatures of concepts which were unavailable to their predecessors. It is part of the story of the development of more sophisticated psychological creatures. It offers a partial explanation of what it is to be more developed, by describing greater internalization or representational capacity in a creature. Internalized expressions included connectives, quantifiers, temporal modifiers, mood-indicators, modal operators, names of psychological states like 'judge' and 'will'. In the Carus lectures and the 'Reply' the procedure was used to deliver legitimated concepts.

At stage 1, some initial concept, like that expressed by the word 'or' or 'not' or 'value', is seen as an extrinsic modifier of a psychological attitude (APA), or as an intuitive but unclarified element of our vocabulary ('Reply'). At stage 2 we reach a specific mental state like "or-thinking" (disjoining), "not-thinking" (rejecting, denying), and "value-thinking" (valuing, approving). These states must be manifested in behavioural responses appropriately connected to the initial concept: for example, "or-judging *A*, *B*" must generate behaviour connected to that of "judging *A* or judging *B*".

At stage 3, reference to these specific states is replaced by a more general psychological verb like 'think' or 'judge', coupled with an operator which appears within, and is restricted to, the scope of the general verb, as in 'thinking *p* or *q*' or 'thinking it valuable to learn Greek'. Only at stage 4 is the restriction removed, so that the operator can appear in subordinate clauses. Grice warns that stage 3 will be apparent and not really distinct from stage 2, that we will have only a notational variant of an expression, unless certain conditions are met. But these conditions differ in his two essays.

In the APA address, what is required to reach a real third stage, for more than notational change, is that an embedded operator must occur within the scope of another embeddable operator. Thus '*x* judges (if *A* or *B*, *C*)'. 'Or-thinking *A* or *B*' is accorded the status of judging that *A* or *B* only when it can be embedded within another operator, here the conditional judgement. But the move from one stage to another must itself, for Grice, be motivated by a theoretical purpose. Grice speculates: there is the demand for a relatively high grade of inference, in which the passage from premisses to conclusion is encompassed, so to speak, within a single thought.

The specific benefit of the procedure described in the APA address is that at stage 3, although we cannot yet claim full objectivity for value (what is thought to be of value lacks syntactico-semantical freedom from being 'thought-that'), judgements of value are not translatable back into preferences or imperatives or any other approving/ volitional attitudes from which they are being constructed. This is arguably due to the more complex linguistic and mental structure in which we find them. It has often been noted that meta-ethical substitutes of favourings and imperatives do not allow for the kind of argumentation which our value judgements permit. Non-translatability does not guarantee that there is no counterpart move in the language of approval for every move in the language of value. It does however put the onus on the anti-objectivist to make out such a claim.

In the 'Reply' Grice requires that one also reach stage 4. Seemingly, it is because 'the permissible complexities [can] be made *intelligible*' (p. 98) only via the provision of something like truth conditions for statements within which the operators appear. Legitimate motivation is demanded as well as truth conditions or their analogues; a point or purpose must be served by invoking a new stage.

In the Carus lectures and the 'Reply', truth conditions or some analogous valuation is called for to reach stage 4. The likely candidate for accreditation is the philosophical story Grice himself tells. This would permit us to attribute to persons, at least, value as members of a kind, where the statement that persons are of value will be detachable from its psychological attitude.

Of course one will think that many other things are of value. To get to the objectivity of those judgements, Grice invokes the following principle: Humean Projection, if performed by a good person in conditions of freedom, allows for the transmission of (absolute, non-relative) value from the person to what seems to him valuable. Grice thought his principle an analogue of the Aristotelian 'what seems good to the good man *is* good.' The principle may be viewed as itself an application of the metaphysical principle of supply and demand; it is a procedure for securing rational demands that is seemingly 'trouble-free'. As rational beings we demand justification for our projects and attitudes; the standards for acceptance do not, however, come ready-made, but must themselves be constructed. Persons, who work at their job, who are concerned to find principles acceptable to rational beings, get the benefits of their job: what seems good to them is.

Grice was amply aware of the problems left unsolved by his account. This introduction will address only two objections it might be natural to raise to the solutions he offered. The first arises from the procedure of Humean Projection, the second concerns both construction routines. One may worry that the application of Humean Projection involves a dangerous circle: value is a suspect term, hence has to be put through the mangle to be legitimated; but it can only be legitimated if we suppose the creature at the mangle to be of absolute value. The 'Reply' offers the means to respond: Grice refers to the principle he once invented, though he did not establish its validity, a principle he labelled *Bootstrap*. 'The principle laid down that when one is introducing the primitive concepts of a theory formulated in an object language, one has freedom to use any battery of concepts expressible in the meta-language, subject to the condition that counterparts of such concepts are subsequently definable or otherwise derivable in the object-language' (p. 93). He could appeal to Bootstrap, to argue that when value as member of a kind is attributed to persons, the term is taken from the theoretician's language, but is viewed as primitive, and unanalysed in the language of humans whose concepts are the object of study. This is legitimate, because it is redeemed once value has been put through the mangle; truth conditions or something analogous having been specified for statements of value.

The second objection contests the legitimating role played by a 'theoretical purpose' and maintains that playing a part in a theory and being objective are quite separate, and that the fact that, for example, persons might be needed for a certain theory does not go very far towards establishing their objectivity. The criticism gets its force from a position taken in the instrumentalist–realist dispute within the philosophy of science. Now there are certain disanalogies in the work and aims of Grice and those disputants which need to be noted at the start, but none the less there is a real issue here, namely, what the difference is between scientific and metaphysical construction, and so what differences with respect to the objectivity of the constructed entities. First, Grice might have been happy if theories of value were 'anti-realist' but had as much objectivity as parts of natural science and mathematics.

Second, the kind of entities which are the focus of the dispute in philosophy of science—unobservable or, better, unobserved entities, are not really the kind of entities which concerned Grice. He once noted in a seminar that some theoretical entities in science, that is, entities inferred but not observed or thought to be observable, have become at a given time observable or recognized to be so. But note that there are two entirely different ways in which this has been held to come about. There is the naïve view, held by some philosophers and the vast majority of microscopists, that successive improvements in instruments have made whole domains of objects observable, starting with sperm and cells in the seventeenth century and, for example, the structure of man-made, integrated circuits on silicon chips in our own day. Then there is the idea, entertained by some philosophers, that if certain theories are true, then objects that we have always been able to observe are identical with what we formerly thought of as unobservable. For example, certain visible crystals are now held to be single molecules, and certain flashes of light are held by NASA to be high-energy electrons. If the scientific theories are correct, and a Kripke-like theory about identity is correct, then we were always able to see some molecules and some electrons.

Evidently what counts as observable is not plain sailing. In the first type of case, in which we extend the limits of observability by making better instruments, it is contingent that we should have become able to observe the sperm or make and observe chips. In the second type of case, on one theory of identity, the flashes are not only identical but also necessarily identical with electrons, but this is known only a posteriori. Grice suggested in contrast a quite different kind of theoretical item, such that it was both necessary that things of that kind should be observable, but also that it could be known a priori, in the course of theory construction, that they should be observable— otherwise they would not fulfil the demands of the theory.

Grice did not propose this curious kind of necessary a priori observability as the distinguishing feature of metaphysically constructed items. It is however tempting and an obvious line to pursue if we confine ourselves to the construction of entities within practical theories. It may be very important for action that persons are directly known and are the kinds of creature that we can know a priori to be directly knowable.

Grice was aware of a need to distinguish scientific from metaphysical construction—what he referred to in the 'Reply' as, respectively, hypothetization and hypostatization. In the 'Reply' he emphasized the importance of construction routines and claimed that we have metaphysical routines of construction, but that there are no such procedures for science, or that when there are, there is a move to metaphysical construction. Grice did not expand on this remark, but it is plausible that the presence of routines is important because there is a difference in who does the constructing; not a small scientific élite, or group of experts, but people in general.

One might, however, still object: although routines may distinguish between the two types of construction, the most we get for our metaphysical entities is justified *acceptance* of them, not true belief. The difference between the two is integral to the dispute. Grice was himself concerned that transcendental or metaphysical argument might establish only the first, and weaker, consequence. Now Grice asserts in the 'Reply' that in some conditions acceptance may confer truth, namely, within the area of metaphysical argument. On the supposition of an intolerable breakdown of rationality if we do not accept a certain thesis, then the demand for acceptance would be sufficient to confer truth on what is to be accepted. 'Proof of the pudding comes from the need to eat it, not vice versa' (p. 96).

Why should we agree to this? We need to see how the argument might go in specific cases to see just what factors are at work. Two features of the earlier example of sheepdogs raise an important question: the new entity, sheepdog, would serve what Grice called a theoretical purpose, permitting us, for example, to explain its behaviour in terms of awareness of its tasks. But at least some of the characteristics which serve as explanation may also be viewed as those presuppositions necessary for any rational agent who works with and trains the animal. They make the agent's action intelligible. Moreover, the rational action in question is a common human activity. Both of these factors help to make it plausible that a new entity has been constructed. The issue they raise here is whether they aren't also underpinnings of the metaphysical argument which threatens a breakdown of rationality. Grice thinks metaphysical arguments are *practical*, that they articulate what are rational demands. The interpretation here is in line with and, I believe, supports this view: the metaphysical argument for the construction of value is indeed practical. For the reconceptions of construction routines arise from our interests and the demands are made from within a practice, from the need to make our common behaviour intelligible. On this interpretation a theoretical purpose may legitimate construction, but only when the construction routine itself is part of a common human activity.

Independently of the appeal to metaphysical argument, Grice has available a second response to the challenge that only necessary acceptance, not truth, is required for his constructions. The routines themselves may be called on to fill the alleged gap between the two. In the example of values, it might be argued that we have both a rational justification for value and the natural tendency to project our attitudes on the world; here there is no gap between justified acceptance of a thesis that there are things of value and belief in its truth. The scientist who accepts a certain constructed entity may be committed to a research programme, to thinking in terms of such an entity. But ontological reservations can have some expression when she is not on her job, when it is not up to her to act as a scientist. Whereas if indeed we value something, our attitude is naturally projected onto the world; it does not result from a commitment nor is it confined to those areas in which action is up to us. Whenever we think of what we value, we have the attitudes and emotions which go with it. What difference could belief in truth bring?

In the closing paragraph of the 'Reply', Grice acknowledged that his defence of value 'bristled' with problems unsolved or incompletely solved. He was avowedly happy rather than dismayed to leave his philosophical friends with work to do.

The Carus Lectures on the Conception of Value

1. VALUE AND OBJECTIVITY

The title which I have chosen for these lectures embodies, as I am sure you will have noticed, an ambiguity of a familiar type, an act object ambiguity. The title-phrase [The Conception of Value] might refer to the item, whatever it may be, which one conceives, or conceives of, when one entertains the notion of value; again, it might refer to the act, operation, or undertaking in which the entertainment of that notion consists, and of which the conception (or concept) of value, in the first sense, is the distinctive object. My introduction of this ambiguity was not accidental: for the precise nature of the connection between, on the one hand, the kind of thinking or mental state which is found, at least in primary instances, when we make attributions of value, and, on the other, the kind of item (if any) which serves as the characteristic object of such thinking is a matter which I regard as quite central to a proper study of the notion of value; my concern with it, moreover, is not an idiosyncrasy, but has been shared by very many of the philosophers who, throughout the ages, have devoted themselves to this topic. Indeed a full understanding of the relationship between this or that fundamental form of thinking and the item, or class of items, which is, or at least might claim to be, a counterpart in extra-mental reality of that form of thinking seems to me a characteristic end of metaphysical enquiry. So it will not, perhaps, surprise you when I suggest, first that one should be ready to pay attention not merely to the *special* [peculiar] character of the central questions about value but also to their *general* character, that is, to their place on the map of philosophical studies and their connection with other questions which are also represented in that map; and second that we should be ready, or even eager, if we can, to provide any answers which may initially find favour in our eyes with a suitable metaphysical backing. To do this might be a way, and might even be the *only* way, to remove the bafflement of certain people (of whom I know several) who are extremely able and highly sophisticated philosophers, particularly in the region of metaphysics, but who say, nevertheless, that they 'really just don't understand ethics'. I suspect that what they are lacking is not (of course) any competence in practical decision-making, but rather a clear picture (if one can be found) of the nature of ethical theorizing and of its proper place in the taxonomy of the enquiries which make up philosophy.

To decide whether and to what extent the kind of global approach which I have in mind would be appropriate in a treatment of fundamental problems about the nature of value, it is obviously desirable to have a reasonably well-defined identification of those problems. To judge from the philosophical literature, prominent among such issues are questions about the objectivity of value (or of values) and questions about the possibility of defending or rebutting scepticism about value (or values); and no sooner has so much been said than it becomes evident that methodological uncertainties arise at the very outset of our investigations. For it is far from clear whether the two sets of questions to which I have just alluded are identical with one another or distinct; are questions about objectivity the same as, or different from, questions about the possible range of scepticism? And if the questions are the same, which way do the identities run? Is the case for scepticism to be equated with the case *for* objectivity, or with the case *against* objectivity?

I myself, in these lectures, plan to pursue my investigation of the conception of value by addressing myself, in the first instance, to questions about objectivity in this region and to the relation of such questions to questions about scepticism. And since my own pre-reflective leanings are in the direction of some form or other of objectivism, I shall, with at least a faint hope of determining whether these leanings are defensible and (indeed) whether they are coherently expressible, begin (but I hope not end) by considering the ideas of two recent anti-objectivists. Today it is the turn of the late J. L. Mackie;[1] tomorrow I shall turn to Philippa Foot.[2]

'There are no objective values' says Mackie (p. 15). Let us try to outline the steps which he takes in order to elucidate and defend this 'bald statement' (as he calls it) of his central thesis concerning the status of Ethics. First of all, he makes it clear that in denying objectivity to values he is not just talking about moral goodness, or moral value (in the strictest sense of that phrase), but it referring to a considerable range of items which could be called "values"; to items which could be 'more loosely called moral values or disvalues', like 'rightness and wrongness, duty, obligation, an action being rotten and contemptible, and so on'; also to an unspecified range of non-moral values, 'notably aesthetic ones, beauty and various kinds of artistic merit.' He suggests that, so far as objectivity is concerned, 'much the same considerations apply to aesthetic and to moral values, and there would be at least some initial implausibility in a view which gave the one a different status from the other'. I find myself in some uncertainty at this point about the extent of the range of values with the status of

[1] [J. L. Mackie, *Ethics: Inventing Right and Wrong* (Harmondsworth, Middlesex, and New York: Penguin Books, 1977), esp. ch. 1. All the quotations from this book were taken without change, with one exception: when quoting from Mackie's p. 17 (p. 31 below), Grice underlined 'not'.]
[2] [Especially 'Morality as a System of Hypothetical Imperatives' in Philippa Foot, *Virtues and Vices and Other Essays in Moral Philosophy* (Berkeley and Los Angeles: University of California Press, 1978).]

which Mackie is concerned, and perhaps partly in consequence of this uncertainty I am not sure whether his
suggestion is that, so far as relates to objectivity, it is
implausible not to assign the same status to moral and to
aesthetic values, or whether it is the seemingly much
stronger suggestion that, so far as relates to objectivity,
plausibility calls for the assignment of the same status to
all values. I shall return to this question.

Mackie envisages three very different reactions to his
initial 'bald statement': that of those who see it as false,
pernicious, and a threat to morality; that of those who see
it as a trivial truth hardly worth mentioning or arguing for;
and finally that of those who regard it as 'meaningless or
empty', as raising no real issue. Before going further into
his elaboration and defence of his anti-objectivist thesis, I
shall find it convenient to touch briefly on his treatment of
the last of these reactions. Mackie (pp. 21–2) associates
this reaction with R. M. Hare, who claimed not to
understand what is meant by "the objectivity of values"
and not to have met anyone who does. Hare's position is
(or was) that there is a perfectly familiar activity or state
called "thinking that some act is wrong" to which
subjectivists and objectivists are both alluding, though the
subjectivist calls this state "an attitude of disapproval"
while the objectivist calls it "a moral intuition"; these are
just different names for the same kind of thing and neither
can be shown to be preferable to the other. As I understand
Mackie's understanding of Hare, this stand-off is ensured
by the fact that the subjectivist has at his disposal a
counterpart move within his own theory for every move
which the objectivist may try to make in order to provide a
distinguishing, and justifying, mark for *his* view of values
as objective. The objectivist, for example, may urge that if
one person declares eating meat to be wrong and another
declares it to be not wrong, they are, both in reality and on
his theory, contradicting each other: to which the subjectivist may retort that though on some subjectivist accounts

they cannot, perhaps, be said to be contradicting each
other, they can be said to be negating (or disagreeing with)
one another: if, for example, one (A) is expressing or
reporting the presence of disapproval of meat-eating in
himself (A), and the other (B) its absence in himself (B),
this would be a case of disagreement or negation; and who
is to say that contradiction rather than "negation" is what
the facts demand? Again, suppose the objectivist claims,
with respect to the persons A and B, one of whom thinks
meat-eating wrong and the other of whom thinks it not
wrong, that he alone (not the subjectivist) is in a position
to assert (as we should wish to be able to assert) that one of
them has to be wrong; Hare's subjectivist, it seems, replies
as follows:

1. Someone (x) thinks that A judges wrongly that meat-
eating is wrong
   - ≡ x disapproves A's judgement that meat-eating is
     wrong
   - ≡ x disapproves A's disapproval of meat-eating
   - ≡ x non-disapproves meat-eating
   $(\rightarrow)^3$

2. Someone x thinks that B judges wrongly that meat-
eating is not wrong
   - ≡ x disapproves B's judgement that meat-eating is
     not wrong
   - ≡ x disapproves B's non-disapproval of meat-eating
   - ≡ x disapproves of meat-eating
   $(\rightarrow)$

3. Any person x must either disapprove or non-
disapprove of meat-eating [disapproval might be either
present or absent in him].[4] So,

   [3] [The arrow appears to be Grice's shorthand way of saying that Hare's
subjectivist could hold all the above assertions to have the same force, or
that some are successively weaker than their predecessors. No matter what
the subjectivist holds on this point, the move from (1), (2), (3), to (4) is
invalid.]
   [4] [Grice took full advantage of the convention of parentheses and
apparently used square brackets for his more important parenthetical
remarks.]

4. Any person x must judge that either A or B judges wrongly.

Hare adds the following further consideration (quoted by Mackie):

> Think of one world into whose fabric values are objectively built, and think of another in which those values have been annihilated. And remember that in both worlds the people in them go on being concerned about the same things—there is no difference in the 'subjective' concern which people have for things, only in their 'objective' value. Now I ask 'what is the difference between the states of affairs in these two worlds?' Can any answer be given except 'None whatever'?

Mackie seems to me not to handle very well this attempt at the dissolution of debates about objectivity. He concentrates on the final invocation of the indistinguishability of the two worlds, the one with and the one without objective values; and he makes three points against Hare. His first comment is that Hare's appeal to the two allegedly indistinguishable worlds does not prove what Hare wants it to prove; all that it does is to underline the point (made by Mackie himself) that it is necessary to distinguish between first-order and second-order ethics, and that the judgements or other deliverances which fall within first-order ethics may be maintained quite independently of any judgement for or against the objectivity of values, which will fall within second-order ethics; it does not show, as Hare would like it to, the emptiness or undecidability of such questions about objectivity. That such questions are not empty is, according to Mackie, indicated by his two further comments; first, that were beliefs in the objectivity of values admissible, they would provide us with a justificatory backing for our valuations, which we shall otherwise be without; and second, that were the world stocked with objective values, we would have available to us a seemingly simple way of acquiring or changing our directions of concern; one could simply let the realities of the realm of values influence one's attitudes, by 'letting one's thinking be controlled by how things were'. Hare's failure to allow for such considerations as these is laid by Mackie at the door of Hare's "positivism", which is comparable with that of a Berkeleian who insists that appearances might be just as they are whether or not a material world lies behind them (or under them).

I am unimpressed. Mackie's first point relies crucially on a deployment of a distinction between first- and second-order ethics which is a central part of this theoretical armament, but whose nature and range of legitimate employment I find exceedingly obscure. I shall postpone further comment until I return to this element in Mackie's apparatus. As for Mackie's other points, "positivism" is, I agree, a bad word, and accusatory applications of it are good for an unreflective giggle. But I suspect that many would regard an unverifiable backing for the propriety of our concerns as being little better than no backing at all. And while it might be held that objective values, should they exist, might exercise an influence on our subjective states, it is by no means clear to me that this is an idea which an objectivist would, or even should, regard with favour. Mackie seems to me, moreover, to have missed the real weakness in Hare's argument (at least, as presented by Mackie). The execution of the second stage of Hare's 'duplication procedure' relies essentially, but not quite explicitly, on the idea that with regard to any particular "content" ϕ, anyone must either disapprove ϕ or not disapprove ϕ. This is indeed, as Hare says, a tautology, but unfortunately it does not entail the premiss which he needs so that his argument will go through; that premiss is that for any ϕ, anyone either has an attitude of disapproval with respect to ϕ or an attitude of non-disapproval with respect to ϕ. This is *not* a tautology, since absence of disapproval only amounts to an *attitude* of non-disapproval if some further condition is also fulfilled, e.g. that the person concerned has *considered* the matter.

The upshot of this discussion is that I am prepared to concede that Mackie is right, though not for the right reasons, when he claims that Hare's attempt to establish that there is no real issue between objectivists and their opponents fails. To make this concession, however, is to condemn only *Hare's attempt to show* that there is no real issue; I remain perfectly free, should further argument point that way, to revive a "dissolutionist" position in a new or modified form. I turn now to the task of trying to identify more precisely the thesis about which objectivists and anti-objectivists are to be supposed to disagree; and I shall start by trying to get clear about what Mackie regards as the thesis which, as an anti-objectivist, he is concerned to maintain. First of all, it is an important part of Mackie's position to uphold the existence of a distinction between first-order and second-order topics (questions, ethical judgements) and to claim that, though both first-order and second-order questions may fall within the province of ethics, his anti-objectivist thesis, like all questions about the status of ethics, is of a second-order rather than a first-order kind. First-order ethical judgements are said to include both such items as evaluative comments about particular actions, and also broad general principles, like the principle that everyone should strive for the general happiness or that everyone should look after himself. By contrast, 'a second-order statement would say what is going on when someone makes a first-order statement, in particular whether such a statement expresses a discovery or a decision, or it may make some point about how we think and reason about moral matters, or put forward a view about the meanings of various ethical terms' (p. 9). Mackie holds there to be a considerable measure of independence between the two realms (first-order and second-order); in particular, "moral scepticism" may belong to either of the two realms and 'one could be a second-order moral sceptic without being a first-order one, or again the other way round. A man could hold strong moral views, and indeed ones whose content was thoroughly conventional, while believing that they were simply attitudes and policies with regard to conduct that he and other people held. Conversely, a man could reject all established morality while believing it to be an objective truth that it was evil and corrupt' (p. 16).

A second salient feature of Mackie's version of anti-objectivism (or moral scepticism) is that it is a *negative* thesis. 'It says that there do *not* exist entities or relations of a certain kind, objective values or requirements, which many people have believed to exist' (p. 17). On some views which have been called objectivist, an objectivist position, despite its positive guise, would turn out to be intelligible only as the denial of some position which would bear the label of "subjectivist", e.g. as the denial of the contention that value statements are reducible to, or really amount to, the expression of certain attitudes like approval or disapproval. On such an interpretation, of the pair of terms, "objectivism" and "subjectivism" (or "non-objectivism", if you like), it would be the latter term which would be, perhaps despite a negative garb, what used to be called in Oxford (with typical artless sexism) the "trouser-word". But, for Mackie, "objectivist" is not a crypto-negative term. A third salient feature is closely related to the foregoing; the assertion or denial of objectivism is not, like some second-order ethical theses, a *semantic* thesis (about the meaning of value terms or the character of value concepts), nor is it a *logical* thesis (e.g. about the structure of certain types of argument), but it is an *ontological* thesis; it asserts (or denies) the existence of certain items in the world of reality. Fourth and last, since Mackie's moral scepticism is proclaimed by him not to be a thesis about the meaning of what moral judgements or value statements assert, but rather about the non-presence of certain items in the real world, it seems to be open to him to hold that the real existence of values is implied by, or claimed in, what ordinary people think and say, but is nevertheless not in fact a feature of the world, with the result that the valuations spoken or thought by ordinary people are systematically and comprehensively *false*. This is in fact Mackie's position; his view is what he calls an "error-view": 'I conclude, then, that ordinary moral judgements include a claim to objectivity, an assumption that there are objective values in just the sense in which I am concerned to deny this' (p. 35). He compares his position with regard to values with that adopted by Boyle and Locke with regard to colours. The suggestion is (I take it) that Boyle and Locke regarded it as a false, vulgar belief that things in the real world possess such qualities as colour; real things do indeed possess certain dispositions to give us sensations of colour, and also possess certain primary qualities (of shape, size, etc.) which are the foundations of these dispositions. But neither of these types of item, which provide explanations for our sensations of colour, is to be *identified* with particular colours, or colour; indeed, *nothing* is to be identified with a particular colour. And the situation with values is analogous.

This leaves us with two questions calling for answers: (1) Why does Mackie hold that claims to objectivity are incorporated in ordinary value judgements? (2) Why does he hold that these claims are false? With regard to the first question, one should perhaps first produce a bit of preliminary nit-picking. Mackie himself wants to hold that a claim to objectivity is incorporated in the ordinary value judgement; such a claim is therefore presumably part of the meaning of such value judgements (or the sentences in which they are expressed); and it does not seem to be, or to be regarded by Mackie as being, a *platitude* that such a claim is included. Mackie cannot therefore consistently assert that his anti-objectivism is not a thesis about the meaning of value averrals; the most he can claim is that though it *contains* a thesis about meaning, it is not *restricted to* a thesis about meaning. More importantly, his view that a claim to objectivity is incorporated in an ordinary value judgement seems to rest, perhaps somewhat insecurely, on his suggestion (pp. 32–4) that there are two leading alternatives to the supposition that it is the function of ordinary value judgements to introduce objective values into discourse about conduct and action: noncognitivism, which (broadly speaking) characterizes value averrals not as statements but rather as expressions of feelings, wishes, decisions, or attitudes; and naturalism, which treats them as making statements about features which are objects of actual or possible desires. Both analyses leave out, and are thought by the ordinary user of moral language to leave out, in one way or another 'the apparent authority of ethics'. The ordinary man's discomfort is relieved only if he is allowed to raise such questions as 'whether this course of action would be wrong in itself. Something like this is the everyday objectivist concept of which talk about non-natural qualities is a philosopher's reconstruction' (p. 34).

Mackie has two arguments, or bundles of argument, on which he relies to support his thesis that the objectivist elements, which according to him are embedded in ordinary value judgements, and in consequence the value judgements which embed them, are false. He calls these arguments *the argument from relativity* and *the argument from queerness*, and considers the second more important than the first. The premiss of the argument from relativity is the familiar range of differences between moral codes from one society to another, from one period to another, and from one group or class to another within a complex community. That there exist these divergences is, according to Mackie, just a fact of anthropology which does not directly support any ethical conclusion, either first-order or second-order. But it may provide indirect support for such conclusions; Mackie suggests that it is more plausible to suppose that moral beliefs reflect ways of life than the other way around: people (in general) approve of monogamy because they live monogamously, rather than live monogamously because they approve of monogamy. This makes it easier to explain the divergences actually found as being the product of different ways of life than as being in one way or another distorted perceptions of objective values. The counter-suggestion that it is open to the objectivist to regard the divergent beliefs as derivative, as the outcome of the operation of a single set of agreed-upon, very general principles on diverse circumstantial assumptions, is dismissed on the grounds that often the divergent beliefs do not seem to be arrived at by derivation from general principles, but seem rather to arise from 'moral sense' or 'intuition'.

The second argument, the 'argument from queerness' consists in an elaboration, along not wholly unfamiliar lines, of the contention that the objectivist, in order to sustain his position, is committed to 'postulating value-entities and value-features of quite a different order from anything with which we are acquainted' and also to attributing to ourselves, in order to render these entities and features accessible to knowledge, a special faculty of moral intuition, a faculty 'utterly different from our ordinary ways of knowing anything else'. In this connection he focuses particularly on the so-called relation of supervenience, which has to be invoked in order to account for the connection of *non-natural* features with natural features, and the dependence of non-natural features upon natural features. The presence of super-venience in particular cases involves the application of a special sort of "because"; 'but just what *in the world* is signified by this "because"?'

Before I try to estimate the merits and demerits of Mackie's position and of the arguments by which he seeks to support it, there seem to me to be two directions of enquiry which are important in themselves, and which could be conveniently attended to at this point, particularly as consideration of them might help to give shape to an evaluation of Mackie. First of all, there are (as Mackie observes) several different possible interpretations of the notion of objectivity, most of them mentioned by him at least in passing, but not all of them ideas which he is concerned to develop or apply. I think it might be useful to enquire what kind or degree of unity, if any, exists between these different readings of the notion of objectivity. Second, I find myself in considerable uncertainty about the connection or lack of connection between attributions (or denials) of objectivity and the adoption (or rejection) of scepticism in one or other of its forms. Does scepticism reside in the camp of the non-objectivist (e.g. Mackie) or in that of the objectivist, or (perhaps) sometimes in one and sometimes in the other?

As regards the notion of objectivity, we have first the interpretation which seems to be the one singled out by Mackie, according to which to ascribe objectivity to a class or category of items is to assert their membership in the company of things which make up reality, their presence in the furniture of the world. We might call this sort of objectivity, *metaphysical* objectivity, and it is the kind of objectivity most commonly supposed to be claimed by realists for whatever it may be that they are realists about. A main trouble with this kind of objectivity is the difficulty in seeing what it is that the objectivist could be claiming; whether, for example, in attributing objectivity to numbers or to material things he is doing anything more than shouting and banging the table as he says 'numbers exist' or 'material things are real.' If the proposition that numbers exist is a consequence of the proposition that there is a number between three and five, what is the objectivist asserting that anyone would care to deny? That numbers (or values) do not just exist, they *really* exist? And what does *that* mean? To escape this quandary, it is not uncommon to take the course which Mackie rejects, namely, to understand 'values (or numbers) are objective' as really negative in character, as a *denial* of the suggestion that values (or numbers) are reducible, by means of one or

another of the possible varieties of reduction, to members
of some class of items which are not values (or numbers),
to (for example) natural features which find favour, or to
classes. Or, maybe, not any and every form of reducibility
would be incompatible with objectivity, but only the kind
of reducibility whose direction is to states of mind,
attitudes, or appearances, to subjective items like approvals
or seeming valuable. An objectivist would now be a
resister, an "anti-dissolutionist", one who seeks to block
certain moves to reach a theoretical simplification or
economy with regard to the constituents of the world. The
objectivist's prime opponent may however be a dissolutionist not in this commodious sense, but in a different and
perhaps even more commodious sense. This opponent may
be one who seeks not to dissolve the target notion (value,
number, material thing, or whatever) into some one or
more different and favoured items or categories of item,
but rather, in one or other of a multitude of diverse ways,
to dissolve the target notion altogether, to dissolve it into
nothing; he may be a *'nihilistic* dissolutionist'. He may
suggest that belief in the application of the target notion is
a *mistake*, one which characteristically or inevitably grips
the unschooled mind; or that such beliefs can claim only
some relativized version of truth (like truth relative to a set
of assumptions, or to a set of standards), not *absolute*
truth. Mackie himself allows to some value judgements
'truth relative to standards', even though by implication he
seems to deny to them "absolute" truth [whatever the
ordinary man may think]. Again, the anti-objectivists may
wish to suggest not that attributions of the target notion
are *mistakes* but rather that they are *inventions*, or perhaps
myths (that is to say, inventions which are backed by
practical motivation, perhaps derived from the utility of
such inventions towards the organization of some body
of material; in the case of values (perhaps) the body of
material might be rules or principles of conduct). As myths
(or as the stuff of which myths are made) they might have

fictive reality, or be "as if" real, without possessing reality proper. Or again, the target notion might be held by the anti-objectivist to be a construct (or a construction): though possessing (or belonging to) reality, values might be held to lack (or fail to inhabit) *primary* or *original* reality; they would belong to an extension of reality provided by *us*. By contrast, an objectivist about values would attribute to them primary or original reality. [I should say at this point that in my view such ideas as are now being raised, that is, distinctions between "as if" or fictive entities, real but constructed entities, and primary or original reality, are among the most important and also the most difficult problems of metaphysics. The obscurity in this area is evidenced by the fact that constructed (non-original) reality might be conceived by some as possessing objectivity and by others as failing to possess objectivity; for some, deficiency in objectivity precludes truth (at least unqualified truth); for others, value claims might be true (in some cases) even though values (as constructed items) lack objectivity.]

It might seem that the wheel, in turning, has now reached the point from which its turning began; for the notion of primitive (unconstructed) reality might be regarded as the same notion as the hazy notion of "out-thereness" or of "being *really* real" which typified the metaphysical objectivist. It might also seem that the new 'interpretation' of objectivity is scarcely if at all less hazy than the earlier one. In an attempt to dispel the mists a little, one might offer the notion of causal efficacy as an index of metaphysical objectivity. Items might be accorded the ribbon of metaphysical objectivity just in case they were capable of acting upon other items, and attributes or features might be regarded as objective just in so far as they were attributes or features in virtue of the possession of which one item would causally influence another, in so far as they helped to explain or account for the operation of such causal influences. A special case of the fulfilment of this condition for objectivity would, in my view, be the capacity, possessed by some objects and some of their attributes, for being perceived, or exercising causal influence on a percipient *qua* percipient. Now the idea of connecting objectivity with causal efficacy seems to me one which has considerable intuitive appeal, indeed much the same kind of appeal as that which may have sustained Dr Johnson in his violent and protracted, though vicarious, assault on Bishop Berkeley. The adequacy, however, of this criterion of objectivity would be seriously, if not fatally, impaired should it turn out that the distinction between what is primitive and what is constructed applies within the scope of causal efficacy—if, that is to say, causal efficacy itself were to be sometimes primitive and sometimes constructed. It is my suspicion that this would indeed turn out to be the case. There would then, perhaps, be no quick recognition-test for objectivity; there would be no substitute for getting down to work and building the theory or system within which the target notion would have to be represented, and seeing whether it, or its representation, does or does not occupy in that theory an appropriate position which will qualify it as objective.

On the approach just considered, then, decisions about the objectivity of a given notion would involve the examination and, if necessary, a partial construction of a theory or system in which that notion (or a counterpart thereof) appears, to see whether within such a system the notion in question (or its counterpart) satisfies a certain condition. The operation of such a decision-procedure would be torpedoed if the requisite theory or system could not be constructed, if the target concept were not theory-amenable. The merits of an allegation that a given notion was not theory-amenable might depend a good deal on what kind of a theory or system was deemed to be appropriate; it would be improper (taking heed of Aristotle) to expect a moralist to furnish a system which allowed for the kind of demonstration appropriate to mathematics.

But one kind of anti-objectivist (who might also be a sceptic) might claim that for some notions *no* kind of systematization was available; in this sense, perhaps, values might not be objective. It may be (as I think my colleague Hans Sluga has argued) that Wittgenstein was both sceptical and anti-objectivist with regard to sensations. In *this* sense of objectivist, an objectivist would only have to believe in theory-amenability; he would not have to believe in the satisfaction, by his target notion, of any further condition within the appropriate systematization.

One further interpretation of objectivity noted by Mackie is one which I shall not pursue today. It connects objectivity with (*so-called*) categorical imperatives as distinct from hypothetical imperatives, and with the (*alleged*) automatic reason-giving force of some valuations. Since this idea is closely related to Miss Foot's theories, I shall defer consideration of it.

I have listed a number of different versions of the idea of objectivity, and have tried to do so in a way which exhibits connections between them, so that the different versions look somewhat tidier than a mere heap. But many of the connections seem to me fairly loose ['such-and-such a notion might be taken as an interpretation of so-and-so'], and I see little reason to suppose many tight, logical connections between one and another version of objectivity.

So much for the panoply of possible interpretations of the notion of objectivity. I turn now to the second of the general directions of enquiry with regard to which I expressed a desire for enlightenment. How is objectivity related to scepticism? Speaking generally, I would incline towards the idea that scepticism consists in doubting or denying something which either *is* a received opinion, or else, at least on the face of it, to some degree *deserves* to be a received opinion. In the present context we are of course concerned only with *philosophical* scepticism; and, without any claim to originality, I would suggest that philosophical sceptics characteristically call in question some highly general class of entity, attribute, or kind of proposition; what they question are categories, or what, if we took ordinary language as our guide, would be categories. To adduce more seeming platitudes, the objectivist is, compared with the anti-objectivist, a metaphysical inflationist; there are more things in *his* heaven and earth than an anti-objectivist Horatio would *allow* himself to dream of. And so, it is standardly thought, it is Horatio who is the sceptic and the objectivist who is the target of scepticism; and (often) Horatio remedies his own initial scepticism by 'reducing' the suspect items to their appearances or semblances: he takes the phenomenalist cure. But here the issue becomes more complex than is ordinarily supposed: for there are to my mind not less than *two* forms of scepticism, which I will call "Whether?" scepticism and "Why?" scepticism. It may be true that the run-of-the-mill objectivist, on account of his inflationary tendencies, provokes "Whether?" scepticism, and that the sceptic who seeks to remedy his own initial scepticism by taking a dose of phenomenalism is not himself open to "Whether?" scepticism. But it may also be true that the phenomenalist is a proper target for "Why?" scepticism; for he has left himself with no way of explaining the phenomena into which he has dissolved the entities or attributes dear to the objectivist. And it may be that the objectivist, if only his favoured entities or attributes were admissible and accessible to knowledge, *would* be in a position to explain the phenomena; and, further, that this capability would be unaffected by the question whether the phenomena are related to possible states of the world (like sensible appearances) or to possible action (like approvals). If only he could be allowed to start, the objectivist could (under one or another interpretation) 'explain' in the one area why it seems that so and so is the case, and in the other why do so and so (e.g. why pay debts).

The foregoing message, that *both* the true-blue, conservative, and inflationary objectivist *and* the red, radical, and deflationary phenomenalist or subjectivist run into a pack of sceptical trouble, of one kind or another, and that more delicate and refined footwork is needed seems to me to be the front-page news in the work of Kant. It also seems to me that Mackie, by being wedded to if not rooted in the apparatus of empiricism, has cut himself off from this lesson. Which is a pity.

However, I must move to somewhat less impressionistic comments on Mackie's position. These comments will fall under three heads:

1. The alleged commitment of 'vulgar valuers', in their valuations, to claims to objectivity.
2. The separation of value judgements into orders, with the assignment to the second order of questions or claims about the status of ethics; and the remediability of an apparent incoherence in Mackie.
3. The alleged falsity of claims of objectivity.

I should say at once that though I think that the considerations which I am about to mention show that something has gone wrong (perhaps that more than one thing has gone wrong) in Mackie's account, the issues raised are so intricate, and so much bound up with (so far as I know) unsolved problems in metaphysics and semantics, that I simply do not know what prospects there might be for refurbishing Mackie's position.

1. It seems to me to be by no means as easy as Mackie seems to think to establish that the 'vulgar valuer', in his valuations, is committed to the objectivity of value(s). It is not even clear to me what *kind* of fact would be needed to establish such a commitment. Perhaps if the vulgar valuer, when making a valuation, (say) that *stealing is wrong*, were to say to himself 'and by "wrong" I mean *objectively wrong*', that would be sufficient (at least if he added a specification of the meaning of "objective"). But nobody, not even Mackie would suppose the vulgar valuer to do

that. Mackie relies, in fact, on the alleged repugnance to the valuer of the two main rivals to an objectivist thesis about value. But even if this were sufficient to show that the vulgar valuer believes in an objectivist thesis about value, it would *not* be sufficient to show that an objectivist interpretation is built into what he *means* when he judges that stealing is wrong. There are other ways of arguing that a speaker is committed to an interpretation, for example, that he has it subconsciously (or unconsciously) in mind, or that what he says is only defensible on that interpretation. But the first direction seems not to be plausible in the present context, and Mackie is debarred from the second by the fact that he holds that what the vulgar valuer says or thinks is not defensible anyway.

To illustrate the fiendish difficulties which may arise in this region, I shall give, in relation to the valuation that stealing is wrong, four different interpretative suppositions—each of which would, I think, have some degree of philosophical appeal—and I shall add in each case an estimate of the impact of the supposition on the assignment of truth value to the valuation.

(*a*) There is a feature W which is objective but provably vacuous of application; a vulgar valuer, when he uses "wrong", is ascribing W. *Conclusion*: vulgar valuation 'stealing is wrong' invariably false.

(*b*) A vulgar valuer thinks (wrongly) that there is a particular feature W which is objective, and when he uses "wrong" he intends to ascribe this feature, even though in fact there is *no* such feature. *Conclusion*: obscure, with choice lying between *false, neither true nor false but a miscue*, and *meaningless* (non-significant).

(*c*) A vulgar valuer is uncommitted about what feature "wrong" signifies; he is ascribing *whatever feature* it should in the end turn out to be that "wrong" signifies. *Conclusion*: assignment of truth value must await the researches of the semantic analyst.

(*d*) A vulgar valuer is uncommitted about what feature "wrong" signifies; truth value is assigned *in advance* of analysis by vulgar methods, and such assignment limits the freedom of the semantic analyst. *Conclusion*: truth value assigned (as stated) by vulgar methods.

2. The idea, to which Mackie subscribes, of separating valuations into orders as a step towards the elucidation of an intuitive distinction between "substantive" and "formal" questions and theses in ethics plainly has considerable appeal; it seems by no means unpromising to regard "substantive" theses about values as being first-order valuations (statements), and to regard "formal" theses in ethics, like theses about the logic of value, or the meaning of value terms, as being a sub-class of second-order theses, and to regard theses about the status of ethics as also falling within this subclass—to treat them, that is to say, as theses *about* first-order valuations. [Such second-order theses, of course, though necessarily *about* valuations, may or again may not themselves *be* valuations.] But Mackie's deployment of this idea plainly runs into trouble. For according to Mackie, vulgar valuations incorporate or entail claims to objectivity; claims to objectivity, according to him, since they fall within, or imply theses belonging to, the class of claims about the status of ethics, are second-order claims; and so, since (presumably) what incorporates or entails a second-order thesis is itself a thesis of not lower than second-order, vulgar valuations are of at least second-order. But vulgar valuations, as paradigmatic examples of substantive value theses, cannot but belong to the *first order*, which is absurd. Now I can suggest an explanation for the appearance on the scene of this incoherence. As I mentioned earlier, among the possible versions of the notion of objectivity are what I called a positive version and a negative version. The positive version, that to attribute objectivity to some item is to proclaim that item

to 'belong to the furniture of the world', is firmly declared by Mackie to be *his* version; and it is, as I have remarked, obscure enough for it to be possible (who knows?) for attributions of objectivity to belong to the first order. The negative version, that to attribute objectivity to something is to deny that statements about that thing are in this or that way eliminable or "reducible", is plainly of second (or higher) order; and despite his forthright assurances, Mackie may have wobbled between these two versions. But to explain is neither to justify nor to remedy: and I have the uneasy feeling that Mackie's troubles have a deeper source than unclarities about application of the notion of order. His "error-view" about value has an Epimenidean ring; it looks a bit as if he may be supposing vulgar valuations to say *of themselves* that the value which *they* attribute to some item or items is objective; and I feel that it may be that such self-reference, though less dramatic, is no less vitiating than would be saying of themselves that they are false. It is true that Mackie regards vulgar valuations as being, in fact, comprehensively false; but it is evident that he expects and wants that falsity to spring from the *general* inapplicability of the attribute being ascribed by such valuations to themselves, not from a *special* illegitimacy attending a valuation's ascription of the attribute *to itself*.

3. I find myself quite unconvinced (indeed unmoved) by the arguments which Mackie offers to support his claim that values are not objective or (should one rather say?) that there are no objective values. The first argument from relativity he regards as of lesser importance than, and indeed as ultimately having to appeal to, the second argument, the argument from queerness. This argument (so it seems to me) seeks to make mileage out of two bits of queerness: first, the queerness of the supposition that there are certain "non-natural" value-properties which are in some mysterious way "supervenient upon" more familiar natural features; and second, the queerness of the supposi-

tion that the recognition of the presence of these non-natural properties motivates us, or *can* motivate us, without assistance from any desire or interest which we happen to have. What strikes *me* as queer is that the queernesses referred to by Mackie are *not* darkly concealed skeletons in objectivist closets which are cunningly dragged to light by him; they are, rather, conditions proclaimed by objectivists as ones which must be accommodated if we are to have a satisfactory theoretical account of conduct, or of other items *qua* things to which value may be properly attributed. So while these queernesses can be used to specify *tasks* which an objectivist could be called upon, and very likely would call on himself, to perform, and while it is not in advance certain that these tasks can be successfully performed, they cannot be used as bricks to bombard an objectivist with even *before* he has started to try to fulfil those tasks. It is perhaps as if someone were to say, 'I seriously doubt whether arithmetic is possible; for if it were possible it would have to be about numbers, and numbers would be very queer things indeed, quite inaccessible to any observation'; or even as if someone were to say, 'I don't see how there can be such a thing as matrimony; if there were, people would have to be bound to one another in marriage, and everything we see in real life and on the cinema-screen goes to suggest that the only way that people can be bound to one another is *with ropes*.'

The Carus Lectures on the Conception of Value

2. RELATIVE AND ABSOLUTE VALUE

My enterprise in this lecture will, initially at least, be to take up and pursue a version of the notion of objectivity which is mentioned by Mackie, but which I have so far deliberately kept out of the limelight. At the conclusion of a short discussion of categorical and hypothetical imperatives, we find (p. 29) the following statement:

So far as ethics is concerned, my thesis that there are no objective values is specifically the denial that any such categorical element (in moral judgments) is objectively valid. The objective values which I am denying would be action-directing absolutely, not contingently (in the way indicated) upon the agent's desires and inclinations.

The language is not wholly clear; but what is seemingly being asserted is that Mackie's denial of objective values is tantamount to a denial that there are any *absolutely* action-directing values, despite what may be claimed in ordinary moral judgements. This thesis seems to be a close relative of a well-known position advanced by Philippa Foot, who has discussed it at some length, and to whom I shall turn my attention in a moment. First, however, let me present the question at issue in a slightly more comprehensive way. There seem to be a number of fairly well-publicized dichotomies, to which the objectivity or non-objectivity of values may be closely related. These include the dichotomy of categorical and hypothetical imperative, the dichotomy of moral value and non-moral value, the dichotomy of absolute value and relative value, and the dichotomy of unconditional and conditional value. The questions at issue seem to me to concern the relation of each of these dichotomies to others in the list. I hope to return to this array of questions after a hopefully succinct presentation of what I take to be Philippa Foot's views.

The following I think would be a fair summary (in *my* language):

1. Hypothetical imperatives are distinguished by the existence of an associated "let out" or "extrication" condition. This will consist in the existence of an associated end, a lack of desire for which will remove from the potential agent all reason to carry out the injunction contained in the imperative. The imperative 'If you want a good dinner, you should eat at the White House' leaves me cold if I have no interest in food.

2. The widespread belief that moral imperatives are categorical, in that they have a reason-giving force that is independent of any desire on the part of the potential agent, is mistaken. There are no such automatic reason-giving forces, and so no categorical imperatives.

3. Though there are no categorical imperatives, there are some "non-hypothetical uses" of "ought", where a disclaimer of interest would have no extricating effect. These occur in "oughts" of etiquette, conduct in games, and possibly (colloquially) in moral statements. But the reason why disclaimers of interest have no effect here is that non-hypothetical uses of ought are (atypically) not reason-giving at all, and so there is here nothing to be extricated *from*.

4. So if moral "oughts" are to be reason-giving at all, they must be interpreted (or re-interpreted) as expressing hypothetical imperatives, depending on some end (like human happiness) which decent people can be counted on to be concerned about.

5. To regard moral precepts as categorical imperatives must be to base morality on reason; anti-moral behaviour

would have to be represented as counter-rational. But there is nothing irrational in immorality; no contradiction or self-defeating behaviour is (characteristically) present.

6. We do not want moral "oughts" to be *ipso facto* motivating or compelling, regardless of interest or inclination or desire. We want volunteers rather than conscripts in moral service.

7. In an earlier version, morality had to be partially justified by reference to the happiness of the agent. In a later version, concern for the welfare of others, *as* part of one's own happiness, demands a *consequential* concern for morality, with a view to the welfare of others.

Now before I get too heavily involved in substantive issues, it might be a good idea for me to pay a little heed to the structural aspects of the region under debate: let us have a look at the girders before covering them with cement. There seem to me to be not less than six dichotomies which are under review, though not every philosopher would regard all of them as well founded. Some philosophers would regard some of them as not distinct from one another, and (I hope) all philosophers would regard some or even all of them as obscure, perhaps even intolerably obscure. These dichotomies are (or include):

1. *objective–non-objective* (or perhaps, *subjective*), (*entity, value*), a dichotomy or cluster of dichotomies on which I have already spent some time.
2. *categorical–hypothetical* (*imperative*)
3. *absolute–relative* (*value*)
4. *moral–non-moral* (*value, imperative*, etc.)
5. *unconditional–conditional* (*value*, etc.)
6. *underived–derived* (*value*)

Today's Special (2. Cats and Hypes), like other members of the bunch, calls (even clamours) for interpretation.

(*a*) A blind logical nose might lead us (or be led) to the assumption of a link between hypothetical imperatives and hypothetical statements (propositions). Such a link no doubt exists, but the most obvious version of it is plainly inadequate. At least one other philosopher besides myself has noticed that 'If he molests the children, you should have him arrested' is unlikely to express a hypothetical imperative; and that even if one restricts oneself to cases in which the antecedent clause specifies a *want*, we find pairs of examples like:

> If you want to go to Chicago, you should travel by AA via Cleveland.
>
> If you want to go to Philadelphia, you should see a psychiatrist.

where it is plain that one is, and the other is not, the expression of a hypothetical imperative (I won't tell you which).

(*b*) A less easily eliminable suggestion, yet one which would still interpret the notion of a "hypothetical imperative" in terms of that particular logical form to which the names "hypothetical" and "conditional" attach, would be the following. Let us assume that it is established, or conceded, as legitimate to formulate conditionals in which not only the consequents (*apodoses*) are couched in some mood (mode) other than the indicative, as in conditional commands ('If you see the whites of their eyes, shoot (fire)') but also the antecedents (*protases*), or some part (clause) of them; in which case all of the following might be admissible conditionals:

> If let the cat be taken to the vet, then let it be put in a cage.
>
> If let the cat be taken to the vet and there is no cage available, then let Martha put it on her lap.
>
> If the cat is sick, let it be taken to the vet.

If this suggestion seems rebarbative, think of these quaint conditionals (when they are quaint) as conditionalized versions of *arguments*, such as

Let the cat go to the vet, so let it be put in a cage.

Let the cat go to the vet; there isn't a cage, so let Martha put the cat on her lap.

and then maybe the discomfort will be reduced.

(*c*) Among conditionals with an imperatival or "volitival" consequent, some will have "mixed" antecedents (partly indicative, partly imperatival) and some will have purely indicative antecedents (like the last of my three examples). I might now give a provisional definition of the terms categorical and hypothetical imperative. A hypothetical imperative is *either* a conditional the consequent of which is imperatival and the antecedent of which is imperatival or mixed (partly indicative, partly imperatival), *or* it is an *elliptical* version of such an imperative. A categorical imperative is an imperative which is either not conditional in form, or else, if it is conditional, has a purely indicative antecedent.

Quick comments:

(i) The structures which I am offering as a way of interpreting hypothetical and categorical imperatives do not, as they stand, offer any room for the appearance of practical modalities like *ought* and *should*, which are so prominently visible in the standard examples of those kinds of imperatives: the imperatives suggested by me are *really* imperatives: they conclude 'do such and such', not 'you/one ought to do such and such'. But maybe my suggestion could be modified to meet the demand for the appearance or occurrence of *ought* (etc.), if such occurrence is needed.

(ii) It would remain to be decided how close the preferred reading of my 'deviant' conditional imperatives would be to the accepted interpretation of standard hypothetical imperatives. But even if there were some divergence, that might be acceptable if the 'new' imperatives turned out to embody a more precise notion than the standard conception.

(iii) There are, I think, serious doubts of the admissibility of conditionals with non-indicative antecedents which will be to my mind connected with the very difficult question whether the indicative and the other moods are co-ordinate, or whether the indicative mood is in some crucial sense *prior* to the other moods. I do not know the answer to this question.

A third interpretation of the distinction between categorical and hypothetical imperatives would, like the first two, be formal in character, and would link the categorical–hypothetical distinction, in relation to imperatives, with one of the other listed dichotomies, that between absolute and relative value. Hypothetical imperatives would be end-relative value attributions, and might be analogous to evidence-relative probabilities; categorical imperatives would not be end-relative. In my eyes this suggestion has the great merit that the idea of the relativization of value might (would) apply to other kinds of relativization than relativization to ends; a notable member of the wider group of relativizations would be relativization to *subjects* of ends, persons who have or who might have ends ("valuable to me"). It is my suspicion that the range of different kinds of relativization is going to prove enormously important in the clarification of the idea of value; it might, for example, turn out that non-relative (absolute) value has some special connection with some favoured relativization of the notion of value (e.g. to people). This third suggestion might help us to see hypothetical and categorical imperatives as important in this context. We might indeed, not inappropriately, use a further member of the original list of dichotomies, the unconditional–conditional value dichotomy, as a means for expressing the distinction between value relative to an end, and value not relative to an end. Then the distinction between absolute and relative value would *include*, as a special case, but would not be *restricted* to, the distinction between unconditional and conditional value.

(*d*) The last interpretation which I shall mention seems *not* to be, as its predecessors were, *formal* in character. It is close to part of what Kant says on this topic, and it also either is or is close to the interpretation employed by Foot. It is a distinction between an imperative being *escapable* (hypothetical), through the absence of a particular desire or concern, and its not being thus escapable (categorical). If we understand the idea of escapability sufficiently widely, the following imperatives are all escapable, even though their logical form is not in every case the same:

> You should give up popcorn.
>
> To get slim, you should give up popcorn.
>
> If you want to get slim, you should give up popcorn.

Now suppose that I have no concern to get slim. One might say that the first imperative is "escaped", provided giving up popcorn has nothing else to recommend it, by being *falsified*. The second and third would not, perhaps, be falsified, but they would, in the circumstances, be *inapplicable* (to me)—and inapplicability, too, counts as escape. Categorical imperatives, however, are in no way escapable.

We should, I suggest, consider not merely imperatives of each sort, together with the range of possible characterizations of the sorts, but also the possible forms of (practical) *argument* into which such imperatives (*particular hypothetical* imperatives) might, on this or that interpretation, enter, and even forms of (practical) argument which involve not hypothetical imperatives themselves, but close relatives of them. To indicate the importance, for a proper understanding of this thorny area, of a consideration of the forms of argument into which they may enter and not merely of the imperatives themselves, I shall give three such patterns of argument, at least superficially different from one another, and (so it seems to me) of varying degrees of breadth of application.

1. (using dichotomy of original–derived value)

   To defend the Philosophy Department would be a good thing. (It is not specified whether the value is original or derived.)

   If to defend the Philosophy Department would be a good thing, then to learn to use bows and arrows would be a good thing (as conducive).

   So: To learn to use bows and arrows would be a good thing. (This would be *derived* value, provided the second premiss is *true*.)

2. It is noble to fight for your country (*unconditional* value).

   It is valuable, in the matter of fighting for one's country, to join one of the services (ascription of *conditional* value).

   So: Join up! (We cannot conclude either to unconditional value of joining up (false) nor to conditional value of joining up, with respect to fighting for one's country, since this is one of the premisses.)

3. It is good for me to increase my holdings in oil shares.

   If I visit my father he will give me some oil shares.

   So: It is good for me to visit my father. (This argument purportedly *transmits* relative value, that is, *subject*-relative value.)

Now where does Foot stand in respect of claims about value?

It seems to me that the issues on which battle has been joined within this topic are always (nearly always) related to different views about the potency of reason (as reflected in the lesser scope or the larger scope allowed for the appearance on the scene of *reasons*). It is by no means clear to me where, precisely, Foot stands in this spectrum (if it matters), but wherever it is, it is somewhere in the middle. The stages which I have in mind are presented in order of *decreasing* scepticism, or *increasing* trust in the power of reason, or, as I would like to be able to put the matter, increasing trust in the legitimate and efficacious operation of the concept of *value* in the conduct of argument.

1. *Thoroughgoing scepticism.* The notion of value has no *genuine* legitimate application in argument; it is never *strictly speaking* the case that one *should* draw such and such a conclusion from a set of premises, that it would be *good* or *valid* to draw such and such a conclusion, or *bad* not to. We do, of course, as victims of bad habits, commonly *talk* that way, and we do, inveterately, throw around the word "reasons", but this is only a way of talking and is not to be taken seriously: it may be hallowed, but it is not at all holy. The things we say are either not to be regarded as true, or if true are true only in some *Pickwickian* sense of the words employed. There are strictly speaking no arguments at all, as (allegedly) it is not too difficult to 'demonstrate'.

2. *Stingy cognitive rationalism.* The terms "value" and "reasons" properly apply, in a non-Pickwickian sense, only within the confines of the area of factual belief, the "alethic" area, and even there only subject to strong safeguards. The only way in which one can find a conclusion validated or called for by reason (subject to reasons) is by finding a case in which to deny rather than accept that conclusion would involve one in *contradiction*.

3. *Open-handed cognitive rationalism.* The crucial terms ("value" and "reason") have a more general licence (inductive reasons are, for example, OK); but strictly legitimate application is still confined to the alethic area.

4. *Limited cognitive-cum-practical rationalism.* The crucial terms have a liberal authentic application in the cognitive (alethic) zone, and also a *limited* authentic application in the practical zone, where they are limited (otherwise than merely as a way of talking) to the area of the relation of means to ends, the area of Aristotelian δεινότης (whatever that area may be).

5. *Unlimited cognitive-cum-practical rationalism.* No types of application are subject to sceptical smear.

Now, as I say, I am not really very sure where Foot stands in this array of stances; I suspect in category 4. I am also fairly sure that wherever Foot may stand, quite a large number of philosophers have occupied, or have thought that they occupied, one of the intermediate positions bearing numbers between 2 and 4 (inclusive). The *further* suspicion which I would like at this point to voice is that the adoption of one of these "part-way" positions is *incoherent*, that you either have to be a whole-hog sceptic or else not a sceptic at all: half-hogging is no good. I shall not attempt to prove this point now; in Lecture 3 I do try to prove a closely related thesis (that if you get as far as stage 4 you have to (in some sense of "have to") go on to stage 5. But there is a stronger and a weaker interpretation of "have to"; the stronger interpretation would allege some form of *contradiction* in accepting 4 but refusing 5, and I rather doubt if *that* can be shown. I have hopes, however, of being able to reach a weaker conclusion, that to accept 4 and to reject 5 (to hold, for example, that hypothetical imperatives are all right, but that categorical imperatives are not) would be wantonly to refuse to satisfy a legitimate rational demand. But for that you must wait patiently for a day.

To initiate a substantive discussion of Foot's position, I ask what there is in it to appeal to us, and again what there is in it to make us hesitate or recoil; and in asking these questions I note that reactions, whether favourable or unfavourable, seem likely to be strong. It seems to me that in these discussions a key role is played by the idea of reason, or of reasons; it will be some set of considerations about reasons which will turn some people on, at least to begin with, and it will be another set of considerations (or possibly even the *same* set of considerations) about reasons which will, at least to begin with, turn other people off. Let us turn first to the considerations which might engender a favourable response.

A central view of Foot's (which might indeed have an extension beyond the realm of the concept of *ought*, so as to apply to a larger range of valuations) is that the primary function (though not its *invariable* function) of the use of an "ought" statement is to produce, or to state the existence of, a reason for a potential agent to perform some specified action or to occupy some specified position or situation. She would go on to say, I think, that it has been, at least since Hume, a commonplace of philosophy that the existence for someone of a reason to perform an action or to occupy a position or situation depends on his having some desire, interest, or disposition of will pointing in that direction; it is objectionable to suppose that there are any features the mere recognition of which is sufficient to provide one with a reason for doing something. The objectionableness of such a supposition may be of either of two kinds; the supposition may be *disbelievable*, or repugnant to the intellect or judgement; or it may be *distasteful*, or repugnant to the will or to inclination. A subsidiary argument of Foot's is, I think, one which would represent the idea that morality consists in a system of categorical imperatives as distasteful, indeed morally distasteful; or at least as less tasteful than the more Humean alternative. We would rather (she suggests) be able to think of people as volunteers in moral service, than be forced to think of them as conscripts, as the more Kantian position would entail.[1]

[1] [The following remarks were included as an aside in the manuscript of the lecture:] The kind of moral (or more or less moral) distaste to which Foot briefly alludes is one which I feel that, as someone brought up in the enlightened 'pinko' (at least on the surface) atmosphere of Oxford, as it used to be, I understand very well. We are in reaction against our Victorian forebears; we are independent and we are tolerant of the independence of others, unless they go too far. We don't like discipline, rules (except for rules of games and rules designed to secure peace and quiet in Colleges), self-conscious authority, and lectures or reproaches about conduct (which are usually ineffective anyway, since those whom they are supposed to influence

Now Foot (an old friend of mine) told me on one of the more recent occasions when we discussed these questions that she had not intended to attach very much weight to her *mot* about 'volunteers and conscripts'. If this is so, then I think that in one pretty important respect she was doing herself an injustice. For whether or not it in fact succeeds on this occasion, it is very much the right *kind* of consideration to bring to bear. In the case of some sorts of valuation, the apparatus for determining whether some particular target should be accorded favourable or un-favourable valuation cannot sensibly be turned upon itself; we cannot sensibly ask whether the apparatus for deter-mining pictorial valuation, or our use of this apparatus, is pronounced by the apparatus itself to be worthy of favourable pictorial valuation, since neither the apparatus nor our use of it is a *picture*. We can ask whether the standards (so far as we can identify them) applied in determining whether something is funny, or our applica-tions of these standards, are themselves licensed as being funny by those very standards: but I very much doubt whether an affirmative answer would be regarded as a significant endorsement of those standards. In other cases—perhaps, for example, with regard to standards of utility—it may well be that a certificate of conformity to these standards, received by the standards themselves or by our use of them, would be properly regarded as an endorsement of the standards. But if, as is the case with moral standards, the standards (in advance of any precise determination of their value) are thought to be *paramount*

are usually either too sensitive or not sensitive enough). Above all we dislike punishment, which only too often just plays into the hands of those who are arrogant or vindictive. We don't much care to talk about "values" (pompous) or "duties" (stuffy, unless one means the duties of servants or the military, or money extorted by the customs people). Our watchwords (if we could be moved to utter them) would be 'Live and let live, though not necessarily with me around' or 'If you don't like how I carry on, you don't have to spend time with me.' With these underlying attitudes, it is not surprising that we don't find Kant congenial, and that we do very much like Strawson's *Freedom and Resentment*.

(not susceptible to being overridden) and it is also the case that the standards endorse themselves or our use of them, then it might, I think, be plausibly suggested that such an endorsement is specially powerful, to the extent that its availability might be taken as a relevant interpretation of the notion of *objectivity*. And an ethical system which failed this test would not have much to hope for beyond a decent burial.

What seems to me wrong with Foot's procedure at this point is not that it is an unsuitable procedure for producing rabbits from hats (it is indeed quite suitable), but that on this occasion it does not produce any rabbits. As one of my colleagues at Seattle (David Keyt) remarked, once you are in one of the services it does not matter whether you are one of the volunteers or one of the conscripts: both are treated alike, and indeed, virtually no one knows which you are. The fact that a consideration is motivating independently of any desire one may have does not imply as a matter either of physical or logical necessity that one in fact acts in line with it; as Kant and others have observed, it is only too obvious that all too often one does not act in line with it. One is not compelled or constrained unless by "constrained"/"compelled" is meant "rationally constrained"/"compelled"—and, as Kant suggested, maybe *that* kind of constraint/compulsion is just what the doctor ordered for the free man.

I turn now to the specification of an attempt to represent the position of Foot's opponent, a champion of 'the received view' which allows a viable distinction between categorical and hypothetical imperatives and seeks to associate moral valuation with categorical imperatives, not as distasteful but as disbelievable. What I have to say has an obvious relation to questions which students in ethics are ready to pose within their first week of classes about whether and how it is possible to justify ends. I am not sure that the considerations with which I shall be concerned are actually voiced by Foot; but that she would assent to them seems to me to be strongly indicated by her view that reasons have to be constituted as such by their connection with desire or interest, and by her refusal (explicitly avowed to me) to countenance such questions as whether, independently of any connection with actual desires, a person *should* have recognized as a reason something which he did not so recognize. I shall take a little trouble to exhibit clearly the structure of the present issue.

It might be suggested that an adherent of the received view is likely to have a certain picture of practical reasoning which is, perhaps, redolent of Aristotle. We decide on the performance of a particular action by ascribing to it a certain value, which is inherited from some state of affairs to which the action would be conducive; the inherited value will be recognized to have descended through a sequence of inheritances, starting from some item whose value is not inherited but original. This picture raises at once hoary problems about how the original value comes to be there and how it comes to be detected. One who adheres to Foot's scheme, however, can lay claim to a capacity to solve or to bypass these difficulties. It is a mistake, he can say, to think of practical reasoning as recognizing the transmission of an original non-relativized value down a chain of inheritors: what we start with is a relativized value (relativized to some person or potential agent), and it is this value which is (sometimes) transmitted. So the question of justifying ends, otherwise than by showing them to be actually desired, does not arise.

The legitimacy of a conception of absolute value, of a kind being denied by the suppositions adherent to Foot's view, is a main topic of my third lecture, and so what I say here should be regarded as having a fairly limited aim. It is designed only to show, or suggest, that *should* it turn out to be theoretically desirable to be able to regard absolute (non-relative) value as attaching to some ends, we should not be at a loss when it comes to saying how such absolute value is to be detected, or how rational decision about ends is possible. While I would not claim to be in a position to give a tidy, comprehensive theoretical account of the matter, it seems to me pretty clear that ordinary agents are thoroughly practised at end-selection. (At this point I draw heavily upon a paper on Happiness which I am prone to deliver, wholly or in part, at every possible opportunity.)

By way of preliminary, three general points seem appropriate.

1. Ends go around in packs or systems; so in determining the suitable ends two linked considerations come into play: the suitability of the end considered as an individual, and also its suitability when it is considered as a member of an actual or potential system of ends (whether in this or that way it does or would *fit in*).

2. Alterations in and institutions of systems of ends normally occur as the outcome of revision; system S' is substituted for system S which is previously ensconced, and what S' and S have in common is much more extensive than the respects in which they differ. As with clothes, changes are mostly matters of patching; and where a new suit is acquired, it is usually ready-made by professional purveyors, like churches or political parties, or private persons like spouses.

3. It is (fortunately for us) possible to make revisions in our system without having to articulate (which we almost certainly would be unable to do) the contents of the system. We can consider a possible change and see what comes to mind, one way or the other, about such a change.

Systems *in situ* seem (not very surprisingly) to be very much like the human beings in whom they are situated. Both change, but in the normal course of events not usually very rapidly: and when changes occur they tend to occur according to natural laws or trends: systems and people grow and develop and sometimes even decay. So when we look for the properties which commend systems, we find them to be not unlike those aspects of *stability* which commend systems of beliefs; which according to Idealists (of the Oxford kind, Bradley, etc.) are such things as coherence, consistency, and comprehensiveness; and it is systems deficient in such respects as these which get modified. Systems which are harmonious, in that the realization of or pursuit of some elements enhances the prospects for other elements, are favoured. So are systems which are (so to speak) teleologically suitable, which bring into play more fully rather than less fully the capacities and attributes which are central to one's constitution as a human being. So, again, are systems which are flexible, which allow for easy and untraumatic revision where revision is required.

When we turn to a consideration of individual ends, we find a variety of procedures which we use to assess the suitability or unsuitability of suggested or possible ends, some of which can also be applied to the assessment of systems of ends. Sometimes we ask whether the adoption of such and such an end would put us at the mercy of circumstances beyond our control; to what extent we should need what Aristotle called *"ektos choregia"* like government grants. Sometimes we enquire about the likely durability of an actual or suggested interest: 'Would we get tired of it?', 'How long would we be capable of sustaining it?', etc. Sometimes we see whether we or someone else can present us with a favourable (or unfavourable) 'picture' of life with such and such as one of our ends. Sometimes we raise second-order questions about the desirability, of one sort or another, of our having some specified item as an end ('Could I be talked into it?', 'Would it be a useful interest to have?', 'Would I look ridiculous if I went in for that?', etc.).

The purpose of this lightning tour of methods of end-assessment has not been to present a systematic account of them, though that would fill a need; it has been intended merely to indicate that so far from being at a loss when it comes to the assessment of ends, we seem to have a wealth of resources at our disposal; so the suggestion that Foot's position has the advantage of enabling us to dispense with such assessment would be to try to pull us out of a hole which we are not in. But there is a further question, namely, whether the methods which we do use for such assessment are more in tune with Foot's position or with a Kantian position. Here I find the outcome not at all clear. It is not at all clear to me how the criteria which we seem to apply in the assessment of ends, and of attachments to them, are to be justified, or even *whether* they are to be justified; and our employment of some of them seems somewhat fluctuating (for example, durability of an interest as something *solid* (and so good), or as *stolid* and so not good). It might turn out that though we evaluate ends, we do not evaluate the criteria by which we evaluate ends; and that might favour Foot. But who knows?

I turn now to a brief delineation of two aspects of Foot's position which seem to have some tendency to make things difficult for her. The first was vividly presented in a talk given by Judy Baker, the relevant passage from which I shall summarize. If I say to you that the door is closed, standardly my purpose in saying this to you is to get you to believe that the door is closed; there are variant descriptions which apply to some cases, like reminding you that the door is closed, letting you know that I am aware that the door is closed, and so on. But it is natural to think of the arousal of a belief as the central case. When I utter a (grammatical) imperative, there is more than one thing I may be doing; if, as a friend watching you shiver, I say 'Close the door' (in a gentle tone of voice, perhaps), I could be *advising* you to shut the door (since you are cold): if, as a parent to a child, I say 'Shut the door', I might be *telling* you to shut the door. There are further distinctions which might be made; for example, we can distinguish between an officer saying to a private soldier, 'Fetch the provisions', when he would be *ordering* the soldier to fetch the provisions, and one private soldier saying to another,

'Fetch the provisions', when he might be *relaying an order* to fetch the provisions. There will be at least two (maybe more) main families of operations, *telling* and *advising*, which will each be further differentiated. All of this is evident to common sense. Now a modalized imperative, like 'You ought to visit your aunt' or 'You mustn't touch the flowers' is perhaps not strictly a recipient of the classifications applicable to unmodalized imperatives, but it is plausible to suppose that assimilation of the modalized imperatives to membership of one or another of the families of imperatives is possible. Now Foot's position seems to demand that moral judgements (valuation, exhortation) should be assimilated to the *advising* family. But this is repugnant to common sense; common sense would support an assimilation to the *telling* family, particularly perhaps to the sub-family of *relaying orders* (in the moral case, from an unspecified and perhaps even unspecifiable source).

Difficulty for Foot may also arise (as Judy Baker also suggested) from her treatment of "non-hypothetical uses", which seem to be represented as "decayed/degenerate cases" of utterances of "ought"—statements (and such-like), which in their primary and non-degenerate employment are dependent on the possession of a certain desire or interest on the part of the addressee or potential agent, but which are here used even though the speaker may not attribute to his addressee such an interest. Examples are etiquette and club rules. The steward may say to a visitor, 'You may not bring ladies into the smoking-room', even though it is obvious that the visitor does not give a fig for the club or its rules. The steward may even say, 'I know you don't care about our rules, but you may not bring ladies into the smoking-room.' The difficulty for Foot is alleged to consist in the fact that we are told that though these are cases in which the original or normal dependence of such utterances on a potential agent's concern or interest has been lost, such injunctions are nevertheless still voiced, perhaps in one or another version of a social routine; we have perhaps got used to saying such things. It is suggested that Foot has not succeeded in making such utterances understandable, from the point of view of the utterer. In particular, while the establishment of social routines or practices is not mysterious, the execution of them has to be thoroughgoing. There would be some inconsistency of behaviour in *including* in a *routine* occurrence of a statement that ladies may not be brought into the smoking-room, a remark to the effect that the addressee does not have the normally requisite interest, which would be an open admission that what is taking place *is* only the operation of a routine or pretence.

Admittedly these objections only show that Foot's position is counter-intuitive, is against what people ordinarily suppose to be the case. It might be none the worse for that. But most of the time Foot seems to want to present herself as coming to the aid of the vulgar valuer, the maker of ordinary moral judgements, in order to protect him against the attempts of the philosophers to read into vulgar valuations material which is not there. It would be uncomfortable to her to have to take the position of condemning (philosophically) what according to her *is* there.

A further difficulty for Foot may arise from this fact that she seems to me to be liable to a charge of having failed to distinguish two different interpretations of phrases of the form "has a reason to" and "has no reason to (for)", and of putting forward a thesis about moral judgements, that they are (or should be) hypothetical imperatives, the attraction of which *depends* on a failure to make this distinction. Suppose that an old lady is struggling up the stairs with a mass of parcels, that I see her, and that I am young, able-bodied, and in no particular hurry. I *could* go and help her to cope, but I do not, because, as I would say, 'What is there in it for me?' I don't care about the minor distresses of old people, and I don't see any likelihood that

I would be rewarded for helping her or penalized for not doing so. On one reading of "have a reason to" it may be that these facts are sufficient to ensure that I have no reason to help her. But helping such people in such circumstances is in fact a matter of ordinary decency and so something we should do. On another reading this may be sufficient to ensure that I have a reason to help her; *there is* a reason for me to help her (its being a matter of ordinary decency), whether or not I recognize the fact; so I *do* have a reason to help her. The charge against Foot would be that the attractiveness of her case for supposing moral imperatives to be hypothetical depends first on equating, perhaps correctly, the application of a moral imperative to a person with his having a reason (perhaps a particular kind of reason) for acting in the prescribed way, and second on attaching to the phrase "having a reason" the first of the two interpretations just distinguished (that in which the man who exhibits indifference towards a given line of action would thereby be shown to lack a reason for such action), thus failing to notice or ignoring the second interpretation, which is the only reading which intuition would allow as adequate for the explication of morality.

Foot might say that she is not confusing the two readings but denying that there is more than the first reading. But she would have to argue for this contention, and it would (I think) be difficult to argue for it in a non-circular way.

I shall conclude this lecture with a brief interim statement, quite undocumented, about where we are and what I might expect to find myself trying to do about it. It seems to me that a whole lot of the trouble that has arisen for Mackie and for Foot has come out of the reluctance of each of them, in this or that degree, to allow full weight to the idea of value as making a bridge between the world of fact and the world of action. It is my suspicion (at the present point no more than a suspicion) that to get our heads clear and keep them clear we shall need to do (at least) five things:

1. To pay unrelenting attention to the intimate connection between reason (the faculty) and reasons, and the intimate association of both with argument and value.

2. To allow for parity, at least in a rational being, of cognition and practical faculties; each is equally guided by reason (rational will), and each alike guides reason (rational will).

3. To take *really* seriously a distinction between rational and pre-rational states and capacities, with unremitting attention to the various relations between the two domains.

4. To recognize value as embedded, in some way yet to be precisely determined, in the concept of a Rational Being. Value does not somehow or another *get in*, it is there from the start.

5. To realize, as one of the fundamental and urgent tasks of philosophy, the need to reach an understanding of the way in which the world ('phenomenal') viewed in terms of cause and effect, and the world ('noumenal') viewed in terms of reasons, fit together (a classical version of the Problem of Freedom).

Perhaps we might, in tomorrow's lecture, move a little way in one or two of these directions.

The Carus Lectures on the Conception of Value

3. METAPHYSICS AND VALUE[1]

The main object of this lecture will be to explore the possibility of providing some kind of metaphysical account of, and positive backing for, the notion of value; and to begin it, I think it would be appropriate for me to voice one or two methodological reflections. But George Myro has told you a story about me, which has indeed the ring of truth; so I shall pause to tell you another story which I hope will ring equally true. When I was still quite a little nipper, my mother gave me a china beer-mug, which I liked enormously; in fact I used it not only to drink beer from, but for a whole lot of other purposes, like carrying gasoline (or as we used to call it, 'petrol') to a neighbour's house when I wanted to set the place on fire. One day I dropped it, and there it lay in fragments. Just at that point my mother appeared on the scene, and reproached me for destroying the mug which she had given me and which I so dearly loved. I said to her, 'Mother [in my family we used to address one another in somewhat formal style], mother, I haven't *destroyed* anything; I have only *rearranged* it a little.' She, being too wise, and insufficiently nimble, to take me on in dialectical jousting, looked at me sadly and said, 'You will have to learn as you grow older.' This

[1] In this lecture I am especially indebted to Richard Warner, without whose timely, skilful, and patient piloting the lecture, and so the series containing it, would not have been written.

encounter, it now seems to me, shaped my later philosophical life; it seems that I *did*, indeed, learn in the end. For first, the metaphysical programme which I shall be seeking to follow will be a *constructivist* programme and not a *reductionist* programme. The procedure which I envisage, if carried out in full, would involve beginning with certain elements which would have a claim to be thought of as metaphysically primary, and then to build up from these starting-points, stage by stage, a systematic metaphysical theory or concatenation of theories. It would be *no* part of my plan to contend that what we end up with 'is *really* only such and suches', or that talking about what my enterprises produce is really only a compressed way of talking about the primary materials, or indeed to make any other claim of that relatively familiar kind. I suspect that many of those who have thought of themselves, like Carnap, as engaged in a programme of construction are really reductionists in spirit and at heart; they would *like* to be able to show that the multifarious world to which we belong reduces in the end to a host of complexes of simple ingredients. That is not my programme at all; I do not want to make the elaborate furniture of the world dissolve into a number of simple pieces of kitchenware; I hope to preserve it in all its richness. I would seek, rather, to understand the metaphysical processes by which one arrives at such richness from relatively simple points of departure. I would not seek to exhibit anything as 'boiling down' to any complex of fundamental atoms.

In order to pursue a constructivist programme of the kind which I have in mind, I will need three things: first, a set of metaphysical starting-points, things which are metaphysically primary; second, a set of recognized construction routines or procedures, by means of which non-primary items are built up on the basis of more primary items; and third, a theoretical motivation for proceeding from any given stage to a further stage, so that the mere possibility of applying the routines would not be itself enough to give one a new metaphysical layer; one would have to have a justification for making that move; it would have to serve some purpose.

The way I imagine myself carrying out this programme in detail (on some day quite a bit longer than today) is roughly as follows. First, I would start by trying to reach a full-dress characterization of what a theory is (an exercise in what I think of as theory-theory); I would be hoping that the specification of what theorizing is would lead in a non-arbitrary way to the identification of some particular kind of theorizing (or theory) as being, relative to all other kinds of theorizing, primary and so deserving of the title of First Theory (or First Philosophy). I would expect this primary theorizing to be recognizable as *metaphysical theorizing*, with the result that a specification of the character and content of metaphysics would be reached in a more systematic way than by just considering whether some suggested account of metaphysics succeeds in fitting our intuitive conception of that discipline. The implementation of this kind of metaphysical programme would, I hope, lead one successively through a series of entities (entity-types), such as a series containing at one stage particulars, followed by continuants, followed by a specially privileged kind of continuants, namely substances, and so on. Each newly introduced entity-type would carry with it a segment of theory which would supplement the body of theory already arrived at, and which would serve to exhibit the central character of the type or types of entity associated with it.

The application of these programmatic ideas to the determination of the conception of value would be achieved in the following way. The notion of value, or of some specially important or fundamental kind of value, like absolute value, would be shown as occupying some indispensable position in the specification of some stage in this process of metaphysical evolution. Such a metaphysical justification of the notion of value might perhaps be comparable to the result of appending, in a suitably integrated way, the *Nicomachean Ethics* as a concluding stage to the *De Anima*. One would first set up a specification of a series of increasingly complex creatures; and one would then exhibit the notion of value as entering essentially into the theory attending the last and most complex type of creature appearing in that series. The un-Carnapian character of my constructivism would perhaps be evidenced by my idea that to insist with respect to each stage in metaphysical development upon the need for theoretical justification might carry with it the thought that to omit such a stage would be to fail to do justice to some legitimate metaphysical demand.

I propose to start today's extract from this metaphysical story at a point at which, to a previously generated stock of particulars which would include things which *some*, though not *all*, would be prepared to count as individual substances, there is added a sequence of increasingly complex items, which (as living things) would be thought of by some (perhaps by Aristotle) as the earliest items on the ascending metaphysical ladder to merit the title of substances *proper*. My first metaphysical objective, at this stage of my unfolding story, would be to suggest a consideration of the not unappealing idea that the notion of *living things* presupposes, and cannot be understood without an understanding of, the notion(s) of purpose, finality, and final cause. In my view this idea is not only appealing but correct; I recognize, however, that there are persons with regrettable deflationary tendencies who would insist that while reference to the notions of finality or final cause may provide in many contexts a useful and illuminating manner of talking about living things, these notions are not to be taken seriously in the metaphysics of biology and are not required in a theoretical account of the nature of life and of living things. A finalistic (or "*vitalistic*") account of the nature of living things might take as a ruling idea (perhaps open to non-vitalists as well) that life consists (very roughly) in the possession of a no doubt interwoven set of capacities the fulfilment, in some degree, of each of which is required for the set of capacities, as a whole, to be retained; a sufficiently serious failure in respect of any one capacity will result in the currently irreversible loss of all the rest; and that would be, as one might say, *death*. The notion of finality might be thought to be unavoidably embedded in the notion of life for more than one reason. One reason would be that if it is in one way or another of the essence of living creatures that one has, instead of an indefinitely extended individual thing, an indefinitely long *sequence* of living things, each individual being produced by, and out of, predecessors in the sequence, then to avoid having individuals which are of outrageous bulk because they contain within themselves the actual bodies of all their descendants, it will be necessary to introduce the institutions of growth and maturity; and with these institutions will come finality, since the states reached in the course of growth and maturity will have to be states to which the creatures aspire and strive, though not necessarily in any conscious way. Another way in which it might be suggested that the notion of finality has to enter will be that at least in a creature of any degree of complexity, the discharge of its vital functions will have to be effected by the operations of various organs or parts, or combinations of such; and each of these organs or parts will have, so to speak, its job to do, and indeed its status as a part (a working functional part, that is to say, and not merely a spatial piece) is determined by its being something which has such-and-such a job or function (eyes are things to see with, feet to walk on, and so forth); and these jobs or functions have to be distinguished by their relation to some feature of the organism as a whole, most obviously to such things as its continued existence. The organism's continuance, though not ordinarily, perhaps, *called* a function of the organism, will nevertheless be required as something which the organism strives for, in order that we should be able to account for the nature of the parts as parts; it will be that thing, or one of the things, to which in their characteristic ways the parts are supposed to contribute. It is worth noting, with regard to the first of these reasons for the appearance of finality on the scene, that for the idea of *actual* containment of a creature within its forebears there is substituted the idea of *potential* containment, an idea which can be extended backwards (so to speak) without any attendant inflation of the bodies of ancestral creatures.

Perhaps I might at this point make two marginal comments on the scheme which I am proposing. First, if I allow myself in discussing the notion of life to ascribe purpose or finality to creatures, parts of creatures, or operations of creatures, such purposes or finalities are to be thought of as detached from any purposers, from any creature or being, mundane or celestial, which consciously or unconsciously *harbours* that purpose or finality. If the walrus or the walrus's moustache has a purpose, that purpose, though it would be the purpose of the walrus, or of its moustache, would not be the walrus's purpose, its moustache's purpose, or even God's purpose. A failure to appreciate this point has been, I think, responsible for some of the disrepute into which *serious* application, within the philosophy of biology, of the concept of finality has fallen. Second, if one relies on finality as a source of explanation (if one does not, what is the point of appealing to it?), if indeed one wishes to use as modes of explanation all, or even more than one, of Aristotle's "Four Causes", one should not be taken to be supposing that there is a single form of request for explanation, a proper response to which will, from occasion to occasion, be now of this type and now of that type, and maybe sometimes of more than one type. It is not that there would be just one kind of "Why?" question with alternative and possibly at times even *rival* kinds of answer; there would be *several* kinds of "Why?" question, different kinds of question being perhaps

linked to categorially different kinds of *candidates* for
explanation, and each kind calling for its own kind of
'cause', its own type of explanation. And it might even be
that, so far from being rivals, different types of 'cause'
worked together, or one *through* another; it might be, for
example, that the operation of final causes demanded and
was only made possible by the operation, say, of efficient
or material causes with respect to a suitably linked
explicandum; the success of a "finality" explanation to a
question asking why a certain organ is present in a certain
kind of organism might depend upon the availability of a
suitable "efficient cause" explanation of how that organ
came to be present.

Nevertheless, these assuaging and anodyne representa-
tions are, I fear, unlikely to appease a dyed-in-the-wool
mechanist. Such a one would be able to elicit from any
moderately sensible vitalist an admission that the mere fact
that the presence of a certain sort of feature or capacity
would be advantageous to a certain type of creature offers
no guarantee that the operation of efficient causes would
in fact provide for the presence of that feature or capacity
in that type of creature. So a vitalist would have to admit
that a "finality" explanation would be non-predictive in
character; and at this point the mechanist can be more or
less counted on to respond that a non-predictive explanation is not really an explanation at all. While a mechanist
might be prepared to allow that survival is a consequence
(in part) of those features which, as one might say, render a
type of creature fit to survive, and perhaps also allow that
this consequence is a *beneficial* consequence, or pay-off,
arising from the presence of those features, he would not
be ready to concede that the creature comes to have those
features *in order that* it should survive. To refine the terms
of this discussion a little: one might try to distinguish
between the question why a certain feature *is* present, and
the question why (or how) that feature *comes to be*
present; the mechanistically minded philosopher might be

represented as doubting whether the first question is intelligible if it is supposed to be distinct from the second, and as being ready to maintain that if, after all, the two questions are distinct and are both legitimate, the provision of an answer to the first cannot be held to *require* the existence of an answer to the second, and indeed is possible at all only given independent information that that feature *has* come to be present.

Furthermore, in respect of other areas where a vitalist (or finalist) is liable to invoke finality as a tool for explanation, the mechanist will say that one can quite adequately explain the phenomena which lead the vitalist to appeal to finality, without having recourse to such an appeal; one will use a particular kind of explanation by efficient causes, one which deploys such cybernetic notions as negative feedback and homoeostasis; as one mechanistic philosopher, David Armstrong, has suggested, people will be like guided missiles.

At this the vitalist might argue that to demand the presence of biological explanation as embodying finalistic apparatus casts no disrespect on the capacity of "prior" sciences (such as physics and chemistry) in a certain sense to explain everything. In a certain sense I can explain why there are seventeen people in the market-place, if in respect of each person who is in the market-place I can explain why he is there, and I can also explain why anyone else who *might* have been in the market-place is in fact somewhere else. But there is an understandable sense in which to do all that does not explain, or at least does not explain *directly*, why there are seventeen people in the market-place. To fill the "explanation-gap", to explain not just indirectly but directly the presence of seventeen people in the market-place, to explain it *qua* being the presence of seventeen people in the market-place, I might have to introduce a new theory, perhaps some highly dubitable branch of social psychology; and I suspect that some scientific theories, like perhaps catastrophe-theory, have arisen in much this kind of way on the backs (so to speak) of perfectly adequate, though not omnipotent, pre-existing theories, in order to explain, in a stronger sense of "explain", things which are already explained in some sense by existing theory.

To this, the mechanist might reply that there is (was) indeed good reason for us to strengthen our explanatory potentialities by adding to the science(s) of physics and chemistry the explanatory apparatus of biology, thus giving ourselves the power to explain directly rather than merely indirectly such phenomena as those of animal behaviour; but it does not follow from that that the apparatus brought to bear by biology should include any finalistic concepts or explanations; explanations given in biological terms are perfectly capable of being understood in cybernetic terms, without any appeal to concepts whose respectability is suspect or in question.

In response to this latest tiresome intervention by the mechanist, I now introduce a reference to something which is, I think, a central feature of the procedures leading to the development of a cumulative succession of theories or theory-stages, each of which is to contain its predecessor. This is the appearance of what I will call *overlaps*. In setting out some theory or theory-stage *B*, which is to succeed and include theory or theory-stage *A*, it may be that one introduces some theoretical apparatus which provides one with a redescription of a certain part of theory *A*. I may, for instance, in developing arithmetic, introduce the concept of positive and negative integers; and if I were to restrict myself to that part of the domain of this 'new' concept which involves solely positive integers, I would have a class of formulæ each of which provides a redescription of what is said by a formula relating to natural numbers; and since the older way of talking (or writing) would be that much more economical, if it came to a fight the natural numbers would win; the innovation would be otiose, since theorems relating solely to positive integers would precisely mirror already available theorems about natural numbers. But of course, to attend in a myopic or blinkered way only to positive integers would be to ignore the whole point of the introduction of the 'new' class of positive and negative integers, which as a whole provides for a larger domain than the domain of natural numbers for a single battery of arithmetical operations, and so for a larger range of specific arithmetical laws. That is the *ratio essendi* of the newly introduced integers, to extend the range of these arithmetical operations. Somewhat similarly, if one paid attention only to examples of universal statements which related to finite classes of objects, one might reasonably suppose the expressions of universal statements to be equivalent to a conjunction of, or to be a 'compendium' of, a set of singular statements; and indeed, at times philosophers have been led by this idea, notably in the case of Mill. But of course, at least part of the point of introducing universal statements is to get beyond the stage at which one is restricted to finite classes, and therefore beyond a stage at which one can regard universal statements as being simply compendia of singular statements.

In the present connection, one might suggest that discourse about detached finality might be regarded as belonging to a system which is an extension or enlargement of a system which confines itself to a discussion of causal connections (efficient or material), including the special kind of causal connections with which cybernetics is concerned; and that this being so, not only is it not surprising but it is positively required, for the extension to be successfully instituted, that finality should enjoy an overlap with some special form of causal connection, like that which is the stock-in-trade of cybernetics. To test the relation between these two conceptual forms (finality and "cybernetical" causal connection), it will be necessary to see whether there is an area beyond the overlap, in which talk about finality is no longer mappable onto talk about caual connection; and the place where it seems to me that it would be natural to look for this divorce to occur, if it occurs at all, would be in the area to which attributions of absolute value belong, and in which talk about finality goes along with attributions of absolute value. If one then denies, as Foot and others have done, that there is *any* metaphysical region in which absolute value is a lawful resident, one seems to be cutting oneself off, maybe not without good reason, from just that testing-ground which is needed to determine the conceptual relationship between finality and causal connection. To this point I shall return.

As I am talking, in this lecture, about finality, I am always referring to what I am calling *detached* finality, that is, to purposes which are detached from any purposer, purposes which can exist without there being any conscious being who has, as *his* purpose, whatever the content of those purposes may be. Now there are some distinctions in relation to finality which I want to make. First, it may be either an essential property of something or an accidental property of it that it has a certain finality. My conception of *essential property* is of properties which are defining properties of a certain sort or kind and also, at one and the same time, intimately bound up with the identity conditions for entities which belong to that kind. [It might indeed be taken as a criterion of a kind's being a *substantial* kind that its defining properties should enter into the identity conditions for its members.] The essential properties of a thing are properties which that thing cannot lose without ceasing to exist (if you like, ceasing to be identical with itself).

It is clear that the *essential* properties of a sort are not to be identified with the *necessary* properties of that sort, the properties which things of that sort must have; for those properties whose presence is guaranteed by logical or metaphysical necessity, given the presence of the essential properties, would not thereby be constituted as essential properties of the sort, that is, as properties which are *constitutive* of the sort. Moreover, attention to the words of Terry Irwin and Alan Code leads me to suspect that in the case of sorts of living things, properties which are essential to a sort might not be invariably present in instances of the sort, and so might fail to be necessary properties of that sort. This possibility, if it is realized, would arise from the fact that membership in a vital sort may be conferred not (or not merely) by character but by ancestry; so a freakish or degenerate instance of such a sort might even lack some essential feature of the sort, provided that its parents or suitably proximate ancestors exhibited that feature.

The link between the two strands in the idea of *essential property*, that of being definitive of a kind and that of constituting an identity condition for members of that kind, becomes eminently intelligible if one takes Aristotle's view that to exist and to be a member of a certain kind are one and the same thing (with appropriate consequences about the multiplicity contained within the notion of being). Now my idea, and I think also the idea of Aristotle, is that the range of essential properties of this or that kind of thing would sometimes, or perhaps even always, include what I might call finality properties, that is, properties which consist in the possession of a certain detached finality.

A second distinction which I want to make is between active and passive finality, a distinction between what it is that, as it were, certain things are supposed to *do*, and (on the other hand) what it is that certain things are supposed to suffer, have done *to* them, have done *with* them, and such-like, including particularly uses to which they are supposed to be put. One might, as a bit of jargon, label the active kind of finality property as *métiers* or *roles*. It would of course be possible, within the area of active finality, to allow for different versions of activity: the activity of a tiger, for example, while legitimately so-called, might be, as one would be inclined to say, activity in a different

'sense of the word' from the activity of a scholar. My idea
would be that every sort of creature, and every individual
belonging to any such sort, must, in virtue of the fact that
it is a sort of living creatures, or a sort of living creature,
possess as an essential property an active finality. To be a
tiger or to be a human being is to possess as an essential
property the capacity to tigerize or the capacity to
humanize, in whatever those things may be thought to
consist.

I will now try to connect up the material which I have
been very sketchily presenting, with the range or corpus of
metaphysical routines or operations which it will be
proper for a metaphysician to deploy in the course of what
I would call the metaphysical evolution of entities or types
of entity. One of these manoeuvres will be, I think, a
manoeuvre which I call Metaphysical Transubstantiation.
There might well be specifically variant forms which this
operation might take, but the central idea would be that
you might have two entity-types (secondary substances)
such that it is perfectly possible for a particular instance of
one type to have exactly the same properties as a particular
instance of another, for them to be in fact indiscernible;
the selection of properties, however, from that total set
which would be essential to an individual entity *qua*
member of one substantial type would not be the same
selection as the selection which would be essential to it *qua*
member of the second type. Therefore it would be a
possibility that something which at one time exhibited the
essential properties of *both* types should at another, later
time exhibit the essential properties of only *one* of these
types. There will be an S_1 which existed both at time t_1 and
at time t_2, and an S_2 which existed at time t_1 when it was
identical with the aforementioned S_1; but at time t_2 the S_2
no longer exists and so of course is not *then* identical with
the S_1. It is this kind of mind-twister which lies at the heart
of Hobbes's problem about the ship and the timber, and
also lies at the centre of what I might call the Grice–Myro

theory of identity, which would allow a thing x and a thing y to be identical at a certain time but to be not identical at a different time, when indeed one of the things may have ceased to exist. Execution of the manoeuvre of Metaphysical Transubstantiation would consist in taking a certain sort of substance S_1, to which a certain property or set of properties P would be essential, and then introducing a type of substance S_2, an instance of which may indeed possess property or properties P, but if it does, does not possess them *essentially*. What will be essential to S_2 will be some other set of properties P', properties which even might attach, though not *essentially*, to some, or even to all, instances of S_1. I am not sure what examples of this manoeuvre are to be found, but the one which I have it in mind to make use of is one in which the manoeuvre is employed to erect, on the basis of the substance-type *human being*, a further substance-type *person*. It is imperative at this point to remember that the general principles of entity-construction, which I adumbrated at the start of this lecture, will dictate that if we are to suppose the manoeuvre to be executed in order to generate, in this way, the substance-type *person*, we must be able to specify an adequate theoretical motivation for the enterprise in which the manoeuvre is employed.

The time has now come to consider the introduction, into a sequence of substantial types being designed by a metaphysician, of the attribute of rationality, which I shall take, when I come to it, as consisting, in the first instance, of a concern on the part of the creature which has it that its acceptances and perhaps (more generally) its attitudes which belong to some specifiable particular class should be well grounded, based on reasons, or (getting closer to the notion of value) *validated*; a concern, that is, on the part of the reason-seeker that the attitudes, positions, and acceptances which he (voluntarily) takes up should have attached to them certificates of value of some appropriate kind. The creature's rationality will consist in the having of this concern together with a capacity, to this or that degree, to give effect to that concern. It will be convenient to consider the introduction of this rationality into a metaphysical scheme in terms of the idea of "construction by a genitor", which I used in an earlier paper.[2] I will ask first why the genitor should be drawn at all towards the idea of adding rationality to any of his sequence of constructed creatures. The answer to that question might be that what he is engaged in constructing are the essential and non-essential features of a sequence of biological types which have to cope with the world and maintain themselves in being, and that a certain range of the exercises of rationality would have biological utility, would improve the chances of a creature which possessed it. One would have to be careful at this point not to go too far, and suppose, for example, that any kind of creature in any kind of circumstances would be biologically improved by the admixture of a dose of rationality: gnats and mosquitoes, for example, might be hindered rather than helped by being rationalized. But rationality might be a biological boon to creatures whose biological needs are complex and whose environment is subject to considerable variation, either because the world is unstable, or because the world though stable combines a high degree of complexity with a reluctance to make easy provisions for its denizens. If a creature's survival depends on the ability to produce differing responses to a vast and varied range of stimuli, then it will become more and more difficult and 'expensive' to equip the creature with a suitably enormous battery of instincts, and the substitution of a measure of rationality will be called for.

Two questions now confront us with regard to the genitor's introduction of rationality. First, is he to be thought of as introducing a relatively unlimited, un-restricted capacity, a capacity perhaps for being concerned about and for handling a general range of "Why?"

[2] [APA Address, pp. 121–61 below; see pp. 140–5.]

questions, or, indeed, simply of *questions*; where the capacity itself is unlimited, though the genitor's *interest* in it is restricted to certain applications of it? Or is he rather to be thought of as introducing a limited *capacity*, a capacity (perhaps) for being concerned about and handling just a small, potentially useful range of questions (just those which are biologically relevant)?

The second question is, is the genitor to be thought of as introducing whatever kind or degree of rationality he does introduce as an *essential* characteristic of the substantial type(s) which he is designing and endowing with it, which we will think of as *Homo sapiens*, or as an *accidental* (non-essential) feature of that type?

To answer these questions in the reverse order, I conjecture, though I cannot establish, that the right procedure is to think of him as introducing rationality as a *non-essential* feature of *Homo sapiens*, though perhaps as a feature which, despite its being non-essential, one can be reasonably assured that instances of *Homo sapiens* will possess. My characteristic candour forces me to admit that I should *like* to be able to find that the genitor would install rationality as an accidental feature, because then there would be scope for a profitable deployment of my new toy, Metaphysical Transubstantiation, the application of which by the genitor would deliver as a constructed substantial type the type *person*, to which rationality could be supposed to belong as an *essential* property; a result which to my mind would be intuitively congenial. But wishful thinking is not an *argument*. Perhaps an argument could be found for attributing to the genitor the seemingly circuitous manoeuvre of first instituting a new biological type (*Homo sapiens*) to which rationality attaches non-essentially though predictably, and then converting this new biological type into a further *non-biological* type (*person*) by a subsequent metaphysical operation which installs rationality as, in this case, an *essential* feature, by reflecting that the programme which in the first instance is engaging the genitor's attention is that of constructing a sequence, or kingdom, of *biological* substantial types, and that rationality is not a feature of the right kind to be a differentiating essential feature in any type falling under *that* programme. If a substantial type is needed to which rationality attaches *essentially*, that type must be generated by a further step.

With regard to the first question, whether the rationality being introduced by the genitor is to be thought of as an unlimited or as a limited capacity, while I think it would be an acceptable general principle that when the genitor wants to achieve a certain objective, of two capacities which would achieve that objective he would (or should) install the weaker capacity on grounds of economy, or so that nothing which he does should be lacking in motivation or deficient with respect to Sufficient Reason, this general principle should not apply to cases in which the weaker capacity could only be generated by initially building a stronger capacity and then subsequently fitting in curbs to restrict the initially installed stronger capacity. Then the suggestion would be that the installation of a limited rationality would be a case of the second kind, achievable only by building in additional special restrictions, and so would be exempted from the scope of the proposed general principle. I think that reaching a decision on this issue would be both rewarding and arduous; and I must regretfully allow the matter to wait.

The way has now been more or less cleared for me to begin to unveil the main idea lying behind this prolonged build-up. This idea is that, given the foregoing assumptions, when the genitor installs rationality into his new substantial type *Homo sapiens* in order to further a biological end, he gets more than he bargained for, in that the newly installed rationality is capable of raising more questions than that limited range of questions in the answering of which the *biological utility* of that rationality at least initially consists. The creature which the genitor creates will not merely be capable of raising and answering a range of questions about how certain ends are to be achieved, of exhibiting, that is, what Aristotle called δεινότης, but will also have both the ability and the requisite concern to raise questions about the desirability or propriety of the ends or results which his rationality enables him to realize. That is to say, the genitor has designed a creature which is capable of asking questions about the value of ends, and so of enquiring about the possible availability of categorical imperatives over and above the hypothetical imperatives which the creature was initially scheduled to deliver. Of course, to say that the creature has the capacity and the concern needed to raise, and desire answers to, certain questions is not to say that the creature is in a position to answer those questions; indeed, we can be sure that initially he will *not* be in a position to answer those questions, since the procedures for getting answers to them have not been designed and installed in advance, and so will have to be evolved or constructed, presumably by *Homo sapiens* himself. But given that such a creature is equipped to formulate a legitimate demand for solutions to these questions, then any set of procedures which it could devise which are such that there is no *objection* to them, and which if they were accepted as proper procedures could then be used to *deliver* answers to these questions, will be procedures which it will be reasonable for the creature to accept *as proper*, provided that there are no other equally unobjectionable candidates with equally good prospects of delivering answers to the same questions.

Should there indeed be two or more sets of procedures, where each set could be put to work, with full success, to provide an answer to a rational demand, and should it be required, for some reason or other, that one and only one such set should be left in the field, and should there be no non-arbitrary way of deciding between the surviving candidates, then I would allow it as rational to decide by the toss of a coin. But I hope to avoid being faced with having to accept so hilarious a mode of decision. I might dub the principle which allows credence to a set of procedures the adoption and use of which will most satisfactorily meet a rational need, "The Metaphysical Principle of Supply and Demand".

The second part of my leading idea would be that, for reasons which have not yet been specified, the newly "generated" creature *Homo sapiens* finds it metaphysically suitable/fitting to perform the operation of Metaphysical Transubstantiation on, so to speak, himself, and to set it up so that the attribution of rationality, which originally (thanks to the genitor) attaches *non-essentially* to *one* substantial type, namely, *Homo sapiens*, now attaches essentially to a different but standardly coincident substantial type, to himself as a person; and that when we come to consider the application of such notions as *value* and *finality* to persons, where the notions of value in question are not questions of relative value but rather of absolute value, then we find that a 'paraphrase' or 'translation' of whatever it is we have to say concerning these notions into some rigmarole or other couched in terms of causal connections of a cybernetic kind is no longer available; and this would be where the end of the overlap is located; when it comes to questions of *absolute* value and about *persons*, the overlap has now ceased. The reasons why the overlap should end at this point might, I suspect, turn on the propriety of supposing persons (essentially rational beings) to be necessarily, and perhaps for that reason, *free*.

Before I fill out the attempted justification for the application of the notion of absolute value on which I have started, I would like to do two things. I would like first to introduce a piece of abbreviatory jargon; and second, I would like to introduce, or reintroduce, a metaphysical construction routine which I referred to in a previous paper,[3] which I called "Humean Projection". The bit of abbreviatory jargon is the phrase "Mechanistically Substitutable"; I shall call an idea or concept "Mechanistically Substitutable" when it is one which initially appears not to be amenable to interpretation in terms agreeable to a mechanist, but which is found to be, after all, so amenable. So for an idea or concept to be *not* mechanistically substitutable would be for it to resist reinterpretation by a mechanist.

As regards "Humean Projection", its title is perhaps somewhat misleading, since though some such operation does seem to be described by Hume, he seemingly regards it as a way of accounting for certain mistakes which we make, of a deep-seated variety, rather than as a way of validating some of the things which we should like to be able to say. In this respect I think we find Mackie going along with Hume. As I see it, this operation consists in taking something which starts life, so to speak, as a specific mode of thinking, and then transforming it into an attribute which is ascribed not to thinking but to the thing thought about and indeed is, in a given case, attributed either correctly or incorrectly. To take an example with which I am presently concerned, we might start with a notion of valuing, or of (hyphenatedly, so to speak) thinking-of-as-valuable some item x; and, subject to the presence of certain qualifying conditions, we should end up with the simple thought, or belief, that the item x is valuable; and in thinking of it as valuable, we should now be thinking, correctly or incorrectly, that the item x has the attribute of being valuable.

I shall now proceed to the amplification of the idea, which I introduced a few minutes ago, of seeking to legitimize, and to secure truth or falsity for, attributions of absolute value by representing such attribution as needed in order to fulfil a rational demand.

---

[3] [APA Address pp. 121–6 below.]

I shall present this amplified version in two parts. The first part is designed to exhibit the structure of the suggestion which is being made and will refer to, without specifying, a certain system of hypotheses, or story, to be called "Story *S*", which is to play a central role in the satisfaction of the aforementioned rational demand. The second part will specify, in outline, Story *S*.

1. The genitor, in legitimately constructing *Homo sapiens* (an operation to which, as genitor, he is properly motivated by a concern to optimize the spread of biological efficiency and so of biological value), will have constructed a creature which will fulfil five conditions:

(*a*) it will legitimately demand justification, ultimately in terms of *absolute* and not *relative* value, for whatever attitudes, purposes, or acceptances (whether alethic or practical) it freely adopts or maintains.

(*b*) it will regard any system of hypotheses, or story, which fulfils the condition of satisfying the afore-mentioned demand ("Demand *D*") without being itself open to objection, as being a story which is worthy of acceptance unless this condition is met by more than one story. (That is, it will regard such a story as a story which is an *admissible candidate* for acceptance.)

(*c*) it will hold that if there is a plurality of admissible candidates *all of which* involve a certain supposition, then that supposition is worthy of acceptance.

(*d*) it will allow that Story *S* is an admissible candidate which meets Demand *D* and that the supposition of the applicability to the world of the notion of absolute value which is embodied in Story *S* would also be embodied in any other story which would satisfy Demand *D*, with the consequence that this supposition is worthy of acceptance.

(*e*) that the notions of *absolute value* and of *finality*, which appear within Story S, are not mechanistically substitutable, and so are authentic and non-Pickwickian concepts.

2. I shall present Story S in the manner of one of those cosy and comforting question-and-answer sequences which telephone companies, public utilities, or insurance companies are liable to give us when they are hoping to unload on us some new gimmick.

Q_1. How can we satisfy Demand D, and get non-relative justification for our purposes, attitudes, and so forth?

A_1. By setting up conditions for the successful application to those purposes, attitudes (etc.) of concept(s) of absolute value.

Q_2. How do we do that?

A_2. By setting it up so that certain sorts of attitudes (etc.) have absolute value inasmuch as they are (or would be) valued by (seem valuable to) a certified value-fixer, whose valuations are (therefore) eligible for the benefits provided by Humean Projection.

Q_3. How do we find one of them?

A_3. We find a being whose essence (indeed whose *métier*) it is to establish and to apply forms of absolute value.

Q_4. How do we get such a being?

A_4. By Metaphysical Transubstantiation from the biological substantial type *Homo sapiens*, which produces for us the non-biological substantial type *person*. We are now seen to be (*qua* persons) accredited value-fixers, at least in relation to ourselves, and (*qua* creatures which are both persons and specimens of *Homo sapiens*) subjects whose voluntary operations are supposed to conform to the values we fix for ourselves.

Q_5. Can we be secured against the risk that the notions of absolute value and of finality, which appear in Story S, might turn out to be mechanistically substitutable (in which case the vitalistic–mechanistic overlap would not after all have been terminated, and the notions in question would after all be 'Pickwickian', not authentic)? A_5. Yes, we can attain this security, provided we can show that being an accredited value-fixer (in relation to oneself) requires being free, in something like Kant's sense of *positive freedom*; and that if the dovetailed concepts of absolute value and finality *were* mechanistically substitutable, this fact would import into the genesis of our self-originated attitudes (etc.) a 'foreign cause' (that is, a cause external to the legislator-cum-agent) which would constitute a barrier to the presence of freedom, and which would for that reason fatally undermine the prospects for success for Story S.

I am only too well aware that today's lecture, particularly in its terminal convulsions, contains much that is obscure, fragmentary, and ill defended (where indeed it is defended at all). I am also conscious of the likelihood that, were I (Heaven forbid) after a breather to return to the fray, I should find myself inclined to produce quite different, though maybe equally problematic, reflections. But I have some hope that today's offering might provide an adequate starting-point for one of those interminable sequences of revisions of which serious theoretical thought seems so largely to consist.

Reply to Richards,[1]
Final Section

METAPHYSICS, PHILOSOPHICAL PSYCHOLOGY, AND VALUE

In this final section of my 'Reply to Richards', I shall take up, or take off from, a few of the things which they have to say about a number of fascinating and extremely import-ant issues belonging to the chain of disciplines listed in the title of this section. I shall be concerned less with the details of their account of the various positions which they see me as maintaining than with the kind of structure and order which, albeit in an as yet confused and incomplete way, I think I can discern in the disciplines themselves and, especially, in the connection between them. Any proper discussion of the details of the issues in question would demand far more time than I have at my disposal; in any case it is my intention, if I am spared, to discuss a number of them, at length, in future writings. I shall be concerned rather to provide some sort of picture of the nature of metaphysics, as I see it, and of the way or ways in which it seems to me to underlie the other mentioned disciplines. I might add that something has already been said in the

---

[1] [The 'Reply to Richards' is Grice's own contribution to the collection of essays in his honour, *Philosophical Grounds of Rationality: Intentions, Categories, Ends*, ed. Richard Grandy and Richard Warner (Oxford: Oxford University Press, 1986). The editors provided a synoptic view of Grice's work, enabling Grice to comment on his own work and interpreta-tions of it in responding to their essay. 'So I make my contribution a response to theirs ... For convenience I fuse the editors into a multiple personality called "Richards", whose multiplicity is marked by the use of plural pronouns and verb-forms' (p. 45).]

previous section of this 'Reply' about philosophical psychology and rationality, and that general questions about value, including metaphysical questions, were the topic of my 1983 Carus lectures. So perhaps I shall be pardoned if here I concentrate primarily on metaphysics. I fear that, even when I am allowed the advantage of operating within these limitations, what I have to say will be programmatic and speculative rather than well ordered and well argued.

At the outset of their comments on my views concerning metaphysics, Richards say, 'Grice's ontological views are at least liberal'; and they document this assertion by a quotation from my *Method in Philosophical Psychology*, in which I admit to a 'taste for keeping open house for all sorts and conditions of entities, just so long as when they come in they help with the housework'. I have no wish to challenge their representation of my expressed position, particularly as the cited passage includes a reference to the possibility that certain sorts of entities might, because of backing from some transcendental argument, qualify as *entia realissima*. The question I would like to raise is, rather, what grounds are there for accepting the current conception of the relationship between metaphysics and ontology? Why should it be assumed that metaphysics consists in, or even includes in its domain, the programme of arriving at an acceptable ontology? Is the answer merely that that enterprise is the one, or a part of the one, to which the term 'metaphysics' is conventionally applied, and so, that a justification of this application cannot be a philosophical issue?

If this demand for a *justified* characterization of metaphysics is to be met, I can think of only one likely strategy for meeting it. That will be to show that success within a certain sort of philosophical undertaking, which I will with striking originality call First Philosophy, is needed if any form of philosophy, or perhaps indeed any form of rational enquiry, is to be regarded as feasible or legitimate; and that the contents of First Philosophy are identical with, or at least include, what are standardly regarded as the contents of metaphysics.[2] I can think of two routes by which this result might be achieved, which might well turn out not to be distinct from one another. One route would perhaps involve taking seriously the idea that if any region of enquiry is to be successful as a rational enterprise, its deliverance must be expressible in the shape of one or another of the possibly different types of theory; that characterizations of the nature and range of possible kinds of theory will be needed; and that such a body of characterization must itself be the outcome of rational enquiry, and so must itself exemplify whatever requirements it lays down for theories in general; it must itself be expressible as a theory, to be called (if you like) Theory-theory. The specification and justification of the ideas and material presupposed by any theory, whether such account falls within or outside the bounds of Theory-theory, would be properly called First Philosophy, and might turn out to relate to what is generally accepted as belonging to the subject-matter of metaphysics. It might, for example, turn out to be establishable that every theory has to relate to a certain range of subject items, has to attribute to them certain predicates or attributes, which in turn have to fall within one or another of the range of types or categories. In this way, the enquiry might lead to recognized metaphysical topics, such as the nature of being, its range of application, the nature of predication, and a systematic account of categories.

A second approach would focus not on the idea of the expressibility of the outcomes of rational enquiry in theories but rather on the question of what it is, in such enquiries, that we are looking for, why they are of concern to us. We start (so Aristotle has told us) as laymen with the awareness of a body of facts; what as theorists we

---

[2] In these reflections I have derived much benefit from discussions with Alan Code.

strive for is not (primarily) further facts, but *rational knowledge*, or *understanding*, of the facts we have, together with whatever further facts our investigations may provide for us. Metaphysics will have as its concern the nature and realizability of those items which are involved in any successful pursuit of understanding; its range will include the nature and varieties of explanation (as offered in some modification of the Doctrine of Four Causes), the acceptability of principles of logic, the proper standards of proof, and so on.

I have at this point three comments to make. First, should it be the case that (1) the foregoing approach to the conception of metaphysics is found acceptable, (2) the nature of explanation and (understood broadly) of causes is a metaphysical topic, and (3) that Aristotle is right (as I suspect he is) that the unity of the notion of *cause* is analogical in character, *then* the *general* idea of cause will rest on its standard particularizations, and the particular ideas cannot be reached as *specifications* of an antecedent genus, for there is no such genus. In that case, *final* causes will be (so to speak) foundation members of the *cause* family, and it will be dubious whether their title as causes can be disputed.

Second, it seems very likely that the two approaches are in fact *not* distinct; for it seems plausible to suppose that explanations, if fully rational, must be systematic and so must be expressible in theories. Conversely, it seems plausible to suppose that the function of theories is to explain, and so that whatever is susceptible to theoretical treatment is thereby explained.

Third, the most conspicuous difficulty about the approach which I have been tentatively espousing seems to me to be that we may be in danger of being given more than we want to receive; we are not, for example, ready to regard methods of proof or the acceptability of logical principles as metaphysical matters, and it is not clear how such things are to be excluded. But perhaps we are in danger of falling victims to a confusion. Morality, as such, belongs to the province of ethics and does not belong to the province of metaphysics. But, as Kant saw (and I agree with him), that does not preclude there being metaphysical questions which arise about morality. In general, there may be a metaphysics of X without it being the case that X is a concept or item which belongs to metaphysics. Equally, there may be metaphysical questions relating to proof or logical principles without it being the case that, as such, proof or logical principles *belong* to metaphysics. It will be fair to add, however, that no distinction has yet been provided, within the class of items about which there are metaphysical questions, between those which do and those which do not belong to metaphysics.

The next element in my attitude towards metaphysics to which I would like to draw attention is my strong sympathy for a *constructivist* approach. The appeal of such an approach seems to me to lie essentially in the idea that if we operate with the aim of expanding some set of starting-points, by means of regulated and fairly well-defined procedures, into a constructed edifice of considerable complexity, we have better prospects of obtaining the explanatory richness which we need than if, for example, we endeavour to represent the seeming wealth of the world of being as reducible to some favoured range of elements. That is, of course, a rhetorical plea, but perhaps such pleas have their place.

But a constructivist methodology, if its title is taken seriously, plainly has its own difficulties. Construction, as normally understood, requires one or more constructors; so far as a metaphysical construction is concerned, who does the constructing? 'We'? But who are we, and do we operate separately or conjointly, or in some other way? And when and where are the acts of construction performed, and how often? These troublesome queries are reminiscent of differences which arose, I believe, among Kantian commentators, about whether Kant's threefold synthesis (perhaps a close relative of construction) is (or was) a datable operation or not. I am not aware that they arrived at a satisfactory solution. The problem becomes even more acute when we remember that some of the best candidates for the title of constructed entities, for example numbers, are supposed to be eternal, or at least timeless. How could such entities have construction dates?

Some relief may perhaps be provided if we turn our eyes towards the authors of fiction. My next novel will have as its hero one Caspar Winebibber, a notorious English highwayman born (or so I shall say) in 1764 and hanged in 1798, thereby ceasing to exist long before sometime next year, when I create (or construct) him. This mind-boggling situation will be dissolved if we distinguish between two different occurrences; first, Caspar's birth (or death), which is dated to 1764 (or 1798), and second, my creation of Caspar, that is to say, my making it in 1985 fictionally true that Caspar was born in 1764 and died in 1798. Applying this strategem to metaphysics, we may perhaps find it tolerable to suppose that a particular great mathematician should in 1968 make it true that (let us say) ultralunary numbers should exist timelessly or from and to eternity. We might even, should we so wish, introduce a 'depersonalized' (and 'detemporalized') notion of construction; in which case we can say that in 1968 the great mathematician, by authenticated construction, not only constructed the timeless existence of ultralunary numbers but also the thereby depersonalized and detemporalized construction of the timeless existence of ultralunary numbers, and also the depersonalized construction of the depersonalized construction of . . . ultralunary numbers. In this way, we might be able, in one fell swoop, to safeguard the copyrights both of the mathematician and eternity.

Another extremely important aspect of my conception of metaphysical construction (creative metaphysical thinking) is that it is of its nature revisionary or gradualist in character. It is not just that, since metaphysics is a very difficult subject, the best way to proceed is to observe the success and failures of others and to try to build further advance upon their achievements. It is rather that there is no other way of proceeding but the way of gradualism. A particular bit of metaphysical construction is possible only on the basis of some prior material; which must itself either be the outcome of prior constructions, or perhaps be something original and unconstructed. As I see it, gradualism enters in in more than one place. One point of entry relates to the degree of expertise of the theorist or investigator. In my view, it is incumbent upon those whom Aristotle would have called 'the wise' in metaphysics, as often elsewhere, to treat with respect and build upon the opinions and the practices of 'the many'; and any intellectualist indignation at the idea of professionals being hamstrung by amateurs will perhaps be seen as inappropriate when it is reflected that the amateurs are really (since personal identities may be regarded as irrelevant) only ourselves (the professionals) at an earlier stage; there are not two parties, like Whigs and Tories, or nobles and the common people, but rather one family of speakers pursuing the life of reason at different stages of development; and the later stages of development depend upon the earlier ones.

Gradualism also comes into play with respect to theory development. A characteristic aspect of what I think of as a constructivist approach towards theory development involves the appearance of what I call 'overlaps'. It may be that a theory or theory-stage *B*, which is to be an extension of theory or theory-stage *A*, includes as part of itself linguistic or conceptual apparatus which provides us with a restatement of all or part of theory *A*, as one segment of the arithmetic of positive and negative integers provides us with a restatement of the arithmetic of natural numbers. But while such an overlap may be needed to secure intelligibility for theory *B*, theory *B* would be pointless unless its expressive power transcended that of theory *A*, unless (that is to say) a further segment of theory *B* lay beyond the overlap. Gradualism sometimes appears on the scene in relation to stages exhibited by some feature attaching to the theory as a whole, but more often perhaps in relation to stages exemplified in some department of, or some category within, the theory. We can think of metaphysics as involving a developing sequence of metaphysical schemes; we can also locate developmental features within and between particular metaphysical categories. Again, I regard such developmental features not as accidental but as essential to the prosecution of metaphysics. One can only reach a proper understanding of metaphysical concepts like *law* or *cause* if one sees, for example, the functional analogy, and so the developmental connection, between *natural* laws and *non-natural* laws (like those of legality or morality). 'How is such and such a range of uses of the word (the concept) *x* to be rationally generated?' is to my mind a type of question which we should continually be asking.

I may now revert to a question which appeared briefly on the scene a page or so ago. Are we, if we lend a sympathetic ear to constructivism, to think of the metaphysical world as divided into a constructed section and a primitive, original, unconstructed section? I will confess at once that I do not know the answer to this question. The forthright contention that if there is a realm of constructs there has to be also a realm of non-constructs to provide the material upon which the earliest ventures in construction are to operate has its appeal, and I have little doubt that I have been influenced by it. But I am by no means sure that it is correct. I am led to this uncertainty initially by the fact that when I ask myself what classes of entities I would be happy to regard as original and unconstructed, I do not very readily come up with an answer. Certainly not common objects like tables and chairs; but would I feel better about stuffs like rock or hydrogen, or bits thereof? I do not know, but I am not moved towards any emphatic 'yes!' Part of my trouble is that there does not seem to me to be any good logical reason calling for a class of ultimate non-constructs. It seems to me quite on the cards that metaphysical theory, at least when it is formally set out, might consist in a package of what I will call ontological schemes in which categories of entities are constructively ordered, that all or most of the same categories may appear within two different schemes with different ordering, what is primitive in one scheme being non-primitive in the other, and that this might occur whether the ordering relations employed in the construction of the two schemes were the same or different. We would then have no role for a notion of *absolute* primitiveness. All we would use would be the relative notion of primitiveness-with-respect-to-a-scheme. There might indeed be room for a concept of authentic or maximal reality; but the application of this concept would be divorced from any concept of primitiveness, relative or absolute, and would be governed by the availability of an argument, no doubt transcendental in character, showing that a given category is mandatory, that a place must be found for it in *any* admissible ontological scheme. I know of no grounds for rejecting ideas along these lines.

The complexities introduced by the possibility that there is no original, unconstructed, area of reality, together with a memory of the delicacy of treatment called for by the last of the objections to my view on the philosophy of language, suggest that debates about the foundations of metaphysics are likely to be peppered with allegations of circularity; and I suspect that this would be the view of any thoughtful student of metaphysics who gave serious attention to the methodology of his discipline. Where are the first principles of First Philosophy to come from, if not from the operation, practised by the emblematic pelican, of lacerating its own breast. In the light of these considerations it seems to me to be of the utmost importance to get clear about the nature and forms of real or apparent

circularity, and to distinguish those forms, if any, which
are innocuous from those which are deadly. To this end I
would look for a list, which might not be all that different
from the list provided by Aristotle, of different kinds, or
interpretations, of the idea of *priority*, with a view to
deciding when the supposition that A is prior to B allows
or disallows the possibility that B may also be prior to A,
either in the same, or in some other, dimension of priority.
Relevant kinds of priority would perhaps include logical
priority, definitional or conceptual priority, epistemic
priority, and priority in respect of value. I will select two
examples, both possibly of philosophical interest, where
for differing m and n, it might be legitimate to suppose that
the priority$_m$ of A to B would not be a barrier to the
priority$_n$ of B to A. It seems to me not implausible to hold
that in respect of one or another version of *conceptual*
priority, the legal concept of *right* is prior to the moral
concept of *right*: the moral concept is only understandable
by reference to, and perhaps is even explicitly definable in
terms of, the legal concept. But if that is so, we are perhaps
not debarred from regarding the moral concept as valua-
tionally prior to the legal concept; the range of application
of the legal concept *ought to be* always determined by
criteria which are couched in terms of the moral concept.
Again, it might be important to distinguish two kinds of
conceptual priority, which might both apply to one and
the same pair of items, though in different directions. It
might be, perhaps, that the properties of sense-data, like
colours (and so sense-data themselves), are posterior in
one sense to corresponding properties of material things
(and so to material things themselves); properties of
material things, perhaps, render the properties of sense-
data intelligible by providing a paradigm for them. But
when it comes to the provision of a suitably motivated
theory of material things and their properties, the idea of
making these *definitionally* explicable in terms of sense-
data and their properties may not be ruled out by the

holding of the aforementioned conceptual priority in the reverse direction. It is perhaps reasonable to regard such fine distinction as indispensable if we are to succeed in the business of pulling ourselves up by our own bootstraps. In this connection it will be relevant for me to reveal that I once invented (though I did not establish its validity) a principle which I labelled as *Bootstrap*. The principle laid down that when one is introducing the primitive concepts of a theory formulated in an object language, one has freedom to use any battery of concepts expressible in the meta-language, subject to the condition that counterparts of such concepts are subsequently definable or otherwise derivable in the object-language. So the more economically one introduces the primitive object-language concepts, the less of a task one leaves oneself for the morrow.

I must now turn to a more direct consideration of the question of how metaphysical principles are ultimately to be established. A prime candidate is forthcoming, namely, a special metaphysical type of argument, one that has been called by Kant and by various other philosophers since Kant a *transcendental argument*. Unfortunately it is by no means clear to me precisely what Kant, and still less what some other philosophers, regard as the essential character of such an argument. Some, I suspect, have thought of a transcendental argument in favour of some thesis or category of items as being one which claims that if we reject the thesis or category in question, we shall have to give up something which we very much want to keep; and the practice of some philosophers, including Kant, of hooking transcendental argument to the possibility of some very central notion, such as experience or knowledge, or (the existence of) *language*, perhaps lends some colour to this approach. My view (and my view of Kant) takes a different tack. One thing which seems to be left out in the treatments of transcendental argument just mentioned is the idea that transcendental argument involves the suggestion that something is being *undermined* by one who is sceptical about the conclusion which such an argument aims at establishing. Another thing which is left out is any investigation of the notion of *rationality*, or the notion of a rational being. Precisely what remedy I should propose for these omissions is far from clear to me; I have to confess that my ideas in this region of the subject are still in a very rudimentary state. But I will do the best I can.

I suspect that there is no single characterization of transcendental arguments which will accommodate all of the traditionally recognized specimens of the kind; indeed, there seem to me to be at least three sorts of argument-pattern with good claims to be dignified with the title of 'transcendental'.

1. One pattern fits Descartes's *cogito* argument, which Kant himself seems to have regarded as paradigmatic. This argument may be represented as pointing to a thesis, namely his own existence, to which a real or pretended sceptic is thought of as expressing enmity, in the form of doubt; and it seeks to show that the sceptic's procedure is self-destructive in that there is an irresoluble conflict between, on the one hand, *what* the sceptic is suggesting (that he does not exist), and on the other hand the possession, by his act of suggesting, of the illocutionary character (being the expression of a doubt) which it not only has but must, on the account, be supposed by the sceptic to have. It might, in this case, be legitimate to go on to say that the expression of doubt cannot be denied application, since without the capacity for the expression of doubt the exercise of rationality will be impossible; but while this addition might link this pattern with the two following patterns, it does not seem to add anything to the cogency of the argument.

2. Another pattern of argument would be designed for use against applications of what I might call 'epistemo-logical nominalism'; that is, against someone who proposes to admit ys but not xs on the grounds that epistemic justification is available for ys but not for anything like xs,

which supposedly go beyond *y*s; we can, for example, allow sense-data but not material objects, if they are thought of as 'over and above' sense-data; we can allow particular events but not, except on some minimal interpretation, causal connections between events. The pattern of argument under consideration would attempt to show that the sceptic's at first sight attractive caution is a false economy; that the rejection of the 'over-and-above' entities is epistemically destructive of the entities with which the sceptic deems himself secure; if material objects or causes go, sense-data and datable events go too. In some cases it might be possible to claim, on the basis of the lines of the third pattern of argument, that not just the minimal categories, but, in general, the possibility of the exercise of rationality will have to go.

3. A third pattern of argument might contend from the outset that if such and such a target of the sceptic were allowed to fall, then something else would have to fall which is a pre-condition of the exercise of rationality; it might be argued, for example, that some sceptical thesis would undermine freedom, which in turn is a pre-condition of any exercise of rationality whatsoever.

It is plain that arguments of this third type might differ from one another in respect of the particular pre-condition of rationality which they brandished in the face of a possible sceptic. But it is possible that they might differ in a more subtle respect. Some less ambitious arguments might threaten a *local* breakdown of rationality, a breakdown in some particular area. An argument might hold, for instance, that certain sceptical positions would preclude the possibility of the exercise of rationality in the practical domain. While such arguments may be expected to carry weight with some philosophers, a really doughty sceptic is liable to accept the threatened curtailment of rationality; he may, as Hume and those who follow him have done, accept the virtual exclusion of reason from the area of action. The threat, however, may be of a *total* breakdown of the possibility of the exercise of rationality; and here even the doughty sceptic might quail, on pain of losing his audience if he refuses to quail.

A very important feature of these varieties of transcendental argument (though I would prefer to abandon the term 'transcendental' and just call them *metaphysical arguments*) may be their connection with practical argument. In a broadened sense of 'practical', which would relate not just to action but also to the adoption of any attitude or stance which is within our rational control, we might think of all argument, even alethic argument, as practical, perhaps with the practical tailpiece omitted; alethic or evidential argument may be thought of as directing us to accept or believe some proposition on the grounds that it is certain or likely to be true. But sometimes we are led to *rational* acceptance of a proposition (though perhaps not to *belief* in it) by considerations other than the likelihood of its truth. Things that are matters of *faith* of one sort or another, like the fidelity of one's wife or the justice of one's country's cause, are typically not accepted on evidential grounds but as demands imposed by loyalty or patriotism; and the arguments produced by those who wish us to have such faith may well not be silent about this fact. Metaphysical argument and acceptance may exhibit a partial analogy with these examples of the acceptance of something as a matter of faith. In the metaphysical region, too, the practical aspect may come first: we must accept such and such a thesis or else face an intolerable breakdown of rationality. But in the case of metaphysical argument, the threatened calamity is such that the acceptance of the thesis which avoids it is invested with the alethic trappings of truth and evidential respectability. Proof of the pudding comes from the need to eat it, not vice versa. These thoughts will perhaps allay a discomfort which some people, including myself, have felt with respect to transcendental arguments. It has seemed to me, in at least some cases, that the most that such arguments could hope to show is that rationality demands the *acceptance*, not the *truth*, of this or that thesis. This feature would not be a defect if one can go on to say that *this* kind of demand for acceptance is sufficient to confer truth on what is to be accepted.

It is now time for me to turn to a consideration of the ways in which metaphysical construction is effected, and I shall attempt to sketch three of these. But before I do so, I should like to make one or two general remarks about such construction routines. It is pretty obvious that metaphysical construction needs to be disciplined, but this is not because without discipline it will be badly done, but because without discipline it will not be done at all. The list of available routines determines what metaphysical construction *is*; so it is no accident that it employs these routines. This reflection may help us to solve what has appeared to me, and to others, as a difficult problem in the methodology of metaphysics, namely, how are we to distinguish metaphysical construction from scientific construction of such entities as electrons or quarks? What is the difference between hypostasis and hypothesis? The answer may lie in the idea that in metaphysical construction, including hypostasis, we reach new entities (or in some cases, perhaps, suppose them to be reachable) by application of the routines which are essential to metaphysical construction; when we are scientists and hypothesize, we do not rely on these routines, at least in the first instance; if at a later stage we shift our ground, that is a major theoretical change.

I shall first introduce two of these construction routines; before I introduce the third I shall need to bring in some further material, which will also be relevant to my task in other ways. The first routine is one which I have discussed elsewhere, and which I call *Humean Projection*. Something very like it is indeed described by Hume, when he talks about 'the mind's propensity to spread itself on objects'; but he seems to regard it as a source, or a product, of confusion and illusion which, perhaps, our nature renders unavoidable, rather than as an achievement of reason. In my version of the routine, one can distinguish four real or apparent stages, the first of which, perhaps, is not always present. At this first stage we have some initial concept, like that expressed by the word 'or' or 'not', or (to take a concept relevant to my present undertakings) the concept of value. We can think of these initial items as, at this stage, intuitive and unclarified elements in our conceptual vocabulary. At the second stage we reach a specific mental state, in the specification of which it is possible, though maybe not necessary, to use the name of the initial concept as an adverbial modifier: we come to 'or-thinking' (or disjoining), 'not-thinking' (or rejecting, or denying), and 'value-thinking' (or valuing, or approving). These specific states may be thought of as bound up with, and indeed as generating, some set of responses to the appearance on the scene of instantiation of the initial concepts. At the third stage, reference to these specific states is replaced by a general (or more general) psychological verb together with an operator corresponding to the particular specific stage which appears within the scope of the general verb, but is still only allowed maximal scope within the complement of the verb and cannot appear in subclauses. So we find reference to 'thinking p or q' or 'thinking it valuable to learn Greek'. At the fourth and last stage, the restriction imposed by the demand that the operators at the third stage should be scope-dominant within the complement of the accompanying verb is removed; there is no limitation on the appearance of the operation in subordinate clauses.

With regard to this routine I would make five observations:

1. The employment of this routine may be expected to deliver for us, as its end-result, *concepts* (in something like a Fregean sense of the word) rather than *objects*. To generate objects we must look to other routines.

2. The provision, at the fourth stage, of full syntactico-

semantical freedom for the operators which correspond to the initial concepts is possible only via the provision of truth conditions, or of some different but analogous valuations, for statements within which the operators appear. Only thus can the permissible complexities be made intelligible.

3. Because of observation 2, the difference between the second and third stages is apparent rather than real. The third stage provides only a notational variant of the second stage, at least unless the fourth stage is also reached.

4. It is important to recognize that the development, in a given case, of the routine must not be merely formal or arbitrary. The invocation of a subsequent stage must be exhibited as having some point or purpose, as (for example) enabling us to account for something which needs to be accounted for.

5. Subject to these provisos, application of this routine to our initial concept ('putting it through the mangle') does furnish one with a metaphysical reconstruction of that concept; or, if the first stage is missing, we are given a metaphysical construction of a new concept.

The second construction routine harks back to Aristotle's treatment of predication and categories, and I will present my version of it as briefly as I can. Perhaps its most proper title would be *Category Shift*; but since I think of it as primarily useful for introducing new objects, new subjects of discourse, by a procedure reminiscent of the linguists' operation of nominalization, I might also refer to it as *subjectification* (or, for that matter, *objectification*). Given a class of primary subjects of discourse, namely substances, there are a number of 'slots' (categories) into which predicates of these primary subjects may fit; one is substance itself (secondary substance), in which case the predication is intra-categorial and *essential*; and there are others into which the predicates assigned in non-essential or accidental predication may fall: the list of these would resemble Aristotle's list of quality, quantity, and so forth.

It might be, however, that the members of my list, perhaps unlike that of Aristotle, would not be fully co-ordinate; the development of the list might require not one blow but a succession of blows; we might, for example, have to develop first the category of attribute, and then the subordinate categories of quantitative attribute (quantity) and non-quantitative attribute (quality), or again the category of event before the subordinate category of action.

Now though substances are to be the *primary* subjects of predication, they will not be the only subjects. Derivatives of, or conversions of, items which start life (so to speak) as predicable, in one non-substantial slot or another, of substances may themselves come to occupy the first slot; they will be qualities of, or quantities of, a particular type or token of substantials: not being qualities or quantities of substances, they will not be qualities or quantities *simpliciter*. (It is my suspicion that only for substances, as subjects, are *all* the slots filled by predicable items.) Some of these substantials which are not substances may derive from a plurality of items from different original categories; events, for example, might be complex substantials deriving from a substance, an attribute, and a time.

My position with regard to the second routine runs parallel to my position with regard to the first, in that here too I hold strongly to the opinion that the introduction of a new category of entities must not be arbitrary. It has to be properly motivated; if it is not, perhaps it fails to be a case of entity-construction altogether, and becomes merely a *way of speaking*. What sort of motivation is called for is not immediately clear. One strong candidate would be the possibility of opening up new applications for existing modes of explanation; it may be, for example, that the substantial introduction of abstract entities, like properties, makes possible the application to what Kneale called 'secondary induction',[3] the principles at work in *primary*

---

[3] William Kneale, *Probability and Induction* (Oxford: Clarendon Press, 1949), 104, for example.

induction. But it is not only the *sort* but the *degree* of motivation which is in question. When I discussed metaphysical argument, it seemed that to achieve reality the acceptance of a category of entities had to be *mandatory*; whereas the recent discussion has suggested that apart from conformity to construction routines, all that is required is that the acceptance be *well motivated*. Which view would be correct? Or is it that we can tolerate a division of constructed reality into two segments, with admission requirements of differing degrees of stringency? Or is there just one sort of admission requirement, which in some cases is over-fulfilled?

Before characterizing my third construction routine I must say a brief word about *essential properties* and about *finality*, two Aristotelian ideas which at least until recently have been pretty unpopular, but for which I want to find metaphysical room. In their logical dress, essential properties would appear either as properties which are constitutive or definitive of a given, usually substantial, kind; or as individuating properties of individual members of a kind, properties such that if an individual were to lose them, it would lose its identity, its existence, and indeed itself. It is clear that if a property is one of the properties which define a kind, it is also an individuating property of individual members of a kind, properties such that if an individual were to lose them, it would cease to belong to the kind and so cease to exist. (A more cautious formulation would be required if, as the third construction routine might require, we subscribed to the Grice–Myro view of identity.) Whether the converse holds seems to depend on whether we regard spatio-temporal continuity as a definitive property for substantial kinds, indeed for *all* substantial kinds.

But there is another, more metaphysical dress which essential properties may wear. They may appear as Keynesian generator-properties, 'core' properties of a substantive kind which co-operate to explain the phenomenal and dispositional features of members of that kind.

On the face of it this is a quite different approach; but on reflection I find myself wondering whether the difference is as large as it might at first appear. Perhaps at least at the level of a type of theorizing which is not too sophisticated and mathematicized, as maybe these days the physical sciences are, the logically essential properties and the fundamentally explanatory properties of a substantial kind come together; substances are essentially (in the 'logical' sense) things such that in circumstances *C* they manifest feature *F*, where the gap-signs are replaced in such a way as to display the most basic laws of the theory. So perhaps, at this level of theory, substances require theories to give expression to their nature, and theories require substances to govern them.

Finality, particularly *detached* finality (functions or purposes which do not require sanction from purposers or users), is an even more despised notion than that of an essential property, especially if it is supposed to be explanatory, to provide us with *final causes*. I am somewhat puzzled by this contempt for detached finality, as if it were an unwanted residue of an officially obsolete complex of superstitions and priestcraft. That, in my view, it is certainly not: the concepts and vocabulary of finality, operating as if they were detached, are part and parcel of our standard procedures for recognizing and describing what goes on around us. This point is forcibly illustrated by William Golding in *The Inheritors*.[4] There he describes, as seen through the eyes of a stone-age couple who do not understand at all what they are seeing, a scene in which (I am told) their child is cooked and eaten by iron-age people. In the description functional terms are eschewed, with the result that the incomprehension of the stone-age couple is vividly shared by the reader. Now finality is sometimes active rather than passive: the finality of a thing then consists in what it is supposed to *do* rather than in

[4] [London: Faber & Faber, 1955.]

what it is supposed to suffer, have done to it, or have done with it. Sometimes the finality of a thing is not dependent on some ulterior end which the thing is envisaged as realizing. Sometimes the finality of a thing is not imposed or dictated by a will or interest extraneous to the thing. And sometimes the finality of a thing is not subordinate to the finality of some whole of which the thing is a component, as the finality of an eye or a foot *may* be subordinate to the finality of the organism to which it belongs. When the finality of a thing satisfies all of these overlapping conditions and exclusions, I shall call it a case of *autonomous* finality; and I shall also on occasion call it a *métier*. I will here remark that we should be careful to distinguish this kind of autonomous finality, which may attach to substances, from another kind of finality which seemingly will not be autonomous, and which will attach to the *conception* of kinds of substance or of other constructed entities. The latter sort of finality will represent the point or purpose, from the point of view of the metaphysical theorist, of bringing into play, in a particular case, a certain sort of metaphysical manœuvre. It is this latter kind of finality which I have been supposing to be a requirement for the legitimate deployment of construction routines.

Now it is my position that what I might call finality features, at least if they consist in the possession of *autonomous* finality, may find a place within the essential properties of at least some kinds of substances (for example, persons). Some substances may be essentially 'for doing such and such'. Indeed, I suspect we might go further than this, and suppose that autonomous finality not merely *can* fall within a substance's essential nature, but indeed, if it attaches to a substance at all, *must* belong to its essential nature. If a substance has a certain *métier*, it does not have to seek the fulfilment of that *métier*, but it does have to be equipped with the motivation to fulfil the *métier* should it choose to follow that motivation. And since autonomous finality is independent of any ulterior end, that motivation must consist in respect for the idea that to fulfil the *métier* would be in line with its own essential nature. But however that may be, once we have finality features enrolled among the essential properties of a kind of substance, we have a starting-point for the generation of a theory or system of conduct for that kind of substance, which would be analogous to the descriptive theory which can be developed on the basis of a substance's essential descriptive properties.

I can now give a brief characterization of my third construction routine, which is called *Metaphysical Transubstantiation*. Let us suppose that the genitor has sanctioned the appearance of a biological type called *humans*, into which, considerate as always, he has built an attribute, or complex of attributes, called *rationality*, perhaps on the grounds that this would greatly assist its possessors in coping speedily and resourcefully with survival problems posed by a wide range of environments, which they would thus be in a position to enter and to maintain themselves in. But, perhaps unwittingly, he will thereby have created a breed of potential metaphysicians; and what they do is (so to speak) to reconstitute themselves. They do not alter the totality of attributes which each of them as a human possesses, but they redistribute them; properties which they possess essentially as humans become properties which as substances of a new psychological type called *persons* they possess accidentally; and the property or properties called rationality, which attaches only accidentally to humans, attaches essentially to persons. While each human is standardly coincident with a particular person (and is indeed, perhaps, identical with that person over a time), logic is insufficient to guarantee that there will not come a time when that human and that person are no longer identical, when *one* of them, perhaps, but not the other, has ceased to exist. But though logic is insufficient, it may be that other theories will remedy the deficiency. Why, otherwise than from a taste for mischief, the humans (or persons) should have wanted to bring off this feat of transubstantiation will have to be left open until my final section, which I have now reached.

My final undertaking will be an attempt to sketch a way of providing metaphysical backing, drawn from the material which I have been presenting, for a reasonably unimpoverished theory of value; I shall endeavour to produce an account which is fairly well ordered, even though it may at the same time be one which bristles with unsolved problems and unformulated supporting arguments. What I have to offer will be close to and I hope compatible with, though certainly not precisely the same as, the content of my third Carus lecture.[5] Though it lends an ear to several other voices from our philosophical heritage, it may be thought of as being, in the main, a representation of the position of that unjustly neglected philosopher Kantotle. It involves six stages.

1. The details of the logic of value concepts and of their possible relativizations are unfortunately visible only through thick intellectual smog; so I shall have to help myself to what, at the moment at least, I regard as two distinct dichotomies. First, there is a dichotomy between value concepts which are *relativized* to some focus of relativization and those which are not so relativized, which are *absolute*. If we address ourselves to the concept *being of value* there are perhaps two possible primary foci of relativization; that of *end* or potential end, that *for* which something may be of value, as bicarbonate of soda may be of value for health (or my taking it of value for my health), or dumb-bells may be of value (useful) for bulging the biceps; and that of *beneficiary* or potential beneficiary, the person (or other sort of item) *to* whom (or to which)

---

[5] [Original Version, 1983; see pp. 69–91 above.]

something may be of value, as the possession of a typewriter is of value to some philosophers but not to me, since I do not type. With regard to this dichotomy I am inclined to accept the following principles. First, the presence in me of a concern for the focus of relativization is what is needed to give the value concept a 'bite' on me, that is to say, to ensure that the application of the value concept to me does, or should, carry weight for me; only if I care for my aunt can I be expected to care about what is of value to her, such as her house and garden. Second, the fact that a relativized value-concept, through a *de facto* or *de jure* concern on my part for the focus of relativization, engages me does not imply that the original relativization has been cancelled, or rendered absolute. If my concern for your health stimulates in me a vivid awareness of the value to you of your medication, or the incumbency upon you to take your daily doses, that value and that incumbency are still relativized *to your health*; without a concern on *your* part for your health, such claims will leave you cold.

The second dichotomy, which should be carefully distinguished from the first, lies between those cases in which a value concept, which may be either relativized or absolute, attaches *originally*, or *directly*, to a given bearer, and those in which the attachment is *indirect* and is the outcome of the presence of a *transmitting* relation which links the current bearer with an original bearer, with or without the aid of an intervening sequence of 'descendants'. In the case of the transmission of relativized value-concepts, the transmitting relation may be the same as, or may be different from, the relation which is embodied in the relativization. The foregoing characterization would allow absolute value to attach originally or directly to promise-keeping or to my keeping a promise, and to attach indirectly or by transmission to my digging your garden for you, should that be something which I have promised to do; it would also allow the relativized value-concept of *value for health* to attach directly to medical care and indirectly or by transmission to the payment of doctor's bills, an example in which the transmitting relation and the relativizing relation are one and the same.

2. The second stage of this metaphysical defence of the authenticity of the conception of value will involve a concession and a contention. It will be conceded that if the only conception of value available to us were that of *relativized* value then the notion of finality would be in a certain sense dispensable; and further, that if the notion of finality is denied authenticity, so must the notion of value be denied authenticity. A certain region of ostensible finality, which is sufficient to provide for the admissibility of attributions of relativized value, is "mechanistically substitutable"; that is to say, by means of reliance on the resources of cybernetics and on the fact that the non-pursuit of certain goals such as survival and reproduction is apt to bring to an end the supply of potential pursuers, some ostensibly final explanations are replaceable by, or reinterpretable as, explanations of a sort congenial to mechanists. But if the concept of value is to be authentic and not merely 'Pickwickian' in character, then it is required that it be supported by a kind of finality which extends beyond the 'overlap' with mechanistically substitutable finality; autonomous finality will be demanded, and a mechanist cannot accommodate and must deny this kind of finality; and so, as will shortly be indicated, he is committed to a denial of absolute value.

3. That metaphysical house-room be found for the notion of absolute value is a *rational demand*. To say this is not directly to offer reason to believe in the acceptability of the notion, though it makes a move in that direction. It is rather to say that there is good reason for *wanting* it to be true that the notion is acceptable. There might be more than one kind of rational ground for this desire. It might be that we feel a need to appeal to absolute value in order to justify some of our beliefs and attributes with regard to

relativized value, to maintain (for example) that it is of absolute value that everyone should pursue, within certain limits, what he regards as being of value to himself. Or again, it might be that, by Leibnizian standards for evaluating possible worlds, a world which contains absolute value, on the assumption that its regulation requires relatively simple principles, is richer and so better than one which does not.

But granted that there is a rational demand for absolute value, one can then perhaps argue that within whatever limits are imposed by metaphysical constructions already made, we are free to rig our metaphysics in such a way as to legitimize the conception of absolute value; what it is proper to believe to be true may depend in part on what one would like to be true. Perhaps part of the Kantian notion of positive freedom, a dignity which as rational beings we enjoy, is the freedom not merely to play the metaphysical game but, within the limits of rationality, to fix its rules as well. In any case, a trouble-free metaphysical story which will safeguard the credentials of absolute value is to be accepted should it be possible to devise one. I have some hopes that the methodology at work here might link up with my earlier ideas about the quasi-practical character of metaphysical argument.

4. On the assumption that the operation of Metaphysical Transubstantiation has been appropriately carried through, a class of biological creatures has been 'invented' into a class of psychological substances, namely persons, who possess as part of their essential nature a certain *métier* or autonomous finality consisting in the exercise, or a certain sort of exercise, of rationality, and who have only to recognize and respect a certain law of their nature, in order to display in favourable circumstances the capacity to realize their *métier*. The degree to which they fulfil that *métier* will constitute them *good persons* ('good *qua*' persons); and while the reference to the substantial kind *persons* undoubtedly introduces a restriction or qualifica-

tion, it is not clear (if it matters) that this restriction is a mode of relativization.

5. Once the concept of *value-qua-member-of-a-kind* has been set up for a class of substances, the way is opened for the appearance of transmitting relationships which will extend the application of value-in-a-kind to suitably qualified non-substantial aspects of members of a kind, such as actions and characteristics. While it cannot be assumed that persons will be the only original instances of value-in-a-kind, it seems plausible to suggest that whatever other original instances there may be will be far less fruitful sources of such extension, particularly if a prime mode of extension will be by the operation of Humean Projection. It seems plausible to suppose that a specially fruitful way of extending the range of absolute value might be an application or adaptation of the routine of Humean Projection, whereby such value is accorded, in Aristotelian style, to whatever would seem to possess such value in the eyes of a duly accredited judge; and a duly accredited judge might be identifiable as a good person operating in conditions of freedom. Cats, adorable as they may be, will be less productive sources of such extension than *persons*.

6. In the light of these reflections, and on the assumption that to reach the goal of securing the admissibility of the concept of absolute value we need a class of primary examples of an unqualified version of that concept, it would appear to be a rational procedure to allot to persons as a substantial type not just absolute value *qua members of their kind*, but absolute value *tout court*, that is to say, *unqualified* absolute value. Such value could be attributed to the kind, in virtue of its potentialities, and to selected individual members of the kind, in virtue of their achievements.

Such a defence of absolute value is, of course, bristling with unsolved or incompletely solved problems. I do not find this thought daunting. If philosophy generated no new problems it would be dead, because it would be finished; and if it recurrently regenerated the same old problems it would not be alive because it could never begin. So those who still look to philosophy for their bread-and-butter should pray that the supply of new problems never dries up.

Method In Philosophical Psychology (From the Banal to the Bizarre)[1]

Preamble

In what follows, I shall be presenting some of my ideas about how I want to approach philosophical psychology. My hope is, in effect, to sketch a whole system; this is quite an undertaking, and I hope that you will bear with me if in discharging it I occupy a little more of your time than is becoming in holders of my august office. While I am sure that you will be able to detect some affinities between my ideas and ideas to be found in recent philosophy, I propose to leave such comparisons to you. Though at certain points I have had my eye on recent discussions, the main influences on this part of my work have lain in the past, particularly in Aristotle, Hume, and Kant. I have the feeling that between them these philosophers have written a great deal of the story, though perhaps not always in the most legible of hands.

---

[1] Presidential Address delivered at the 49th Annual Meeting of the American Philosophical Association in San Diego, 28 March 1975. Earlier versions of this address were given in lectures at Princeton University in March 1972, and as a John Dewey lecture at the University of Michigan in Ann Arbor in April 1974.

I. Some Focal Problems

I shall begin by formulating, in outline, a sequence of four particular problems which I think an adequate philosophical psychology must be able to lay to rest.

The first problem (Problem A) concerns the real or apparent circularity with which one is liable to be faced if one attempts to provide an analysis of central psychological concepts by means of explicit definitions. Suppose that, like some philosophers of the not so distant past, we are attracted by the idea of giving dispositional behaviouristic analyses of such concepts, and that we make a start on the concept of belief. As a first shot, we try the following, B_1: x believes that p just in case x is disposed to act as if p were true. In response to obvious queries about the meaning of the phrase, 'act as if p were true', we substitute, for B_1, B_2: x believes that p just in case x is disposed, whenever x wants (desires) some end E, to act in ways which will realize E given that p is true rather than in ways which will realize E given that p is false. The precise form which such a definition as B_2 might take is immaterial to my present purpose, provided that it has two features observable in B_2; first, that a further psychological concept, that of wanting, has been introduced in the definiens; and second, that to meet another obvious response, the concept of belief itself has to be reintroduced in the definiens. For the disposition associated with a belief that p surely should be specified, not as a disposition to act in ways which will *in fact* realize E given that p is true, but rather as a disposition to act in ways which x *believes* will, given that p is true, realize E. One who believes that p may often fail to act in ways that would realize E given that p were true, because he is quite unaware of the fact that such actions would realize E if p were true; and he may quite often act in ways which would realize E only if p were false, because he mistakenly *believes* that such ways would realize E if p were true.

If we turn to the concept of wanting, which B_2 introduced into the definiens for belief, we seem to encounter a parallel situation. Suppose we start with W_1: x wants E just in case x is disposed to act in ways which will realize E rather than in ways which will realize the negation of E. Precisely the same kind of objection as that just raised in the case of belief seems to compel the introduction of the concept of belief into the definiens of W_1 giving us W_2: x wants E just in case x is disposed to act in ways which x *believes* will realize E rather than in ways which x *believes* will realize the negation of E. We now meet the further objection that one who wants E can be counted on to act in such ways as these only provided that there is no E' which he wants more than E; if there is such an E', then in any situation in which E' conflicts with E he may be expected to act in ways he thinks will realize the negation of E. But the incorporation of any version of this proviso into the definiens for wanting will reintroduce the concept of wanting itself.

The situation, then, seems to be that if, along the envisaged behaviouristic lines, we attempt to provide explicit definitions for such a pair of concepts as those of belief and wanting, whichever member of the pair we start with we are driven into the very small circle of introducing into the definiens the very concept which is being defined, and also into the slightly larger circle of introducing into the definiens the other member of the pair. The idea suggested to me by this difficulty is that we might be well advised, as a first move, to abandon the idea of looking for *explicit* definitions of central psychological concepts, and look instead for *implicit* definitions, to be provided by some form of axiomatic treatment; leaving open the possibility that, as a second move, this kind of treatment might be made the foundation for a different sort of explicit definition. Such a procedure might well preserve an attractive feature of behaviouristic analyses, that of attempting to explain psychological concepts by relating them to appropriate forms of behaviour, while at the same time freeing us from the logical embarrassments into which such analyses seem to lead us.

We are now, however, faced with a further question: if we are to think of certain psychological concepts as being implicitly defined by some set of laws (or quasi-laws) in which they figure, are we to attribute to such laws a contingent or a non-contingent status? A look at some strong candidates for the position of being laws of the kind which we are seeking seems merely to reinforce the question. Consider the principle 'He who wills the end wills the means,' some form of which seems to me to be the idea behind both of the behaviouristic definitions just discussed; and interpret it as saying that anyone who wills some end, and also believes that some action on his part is an indispensable means to that end, wills the action in question. One might be inclined to say that if anyone believed (*really* believed) that a certain line of action was indispensable to the attainment of a certain end, and yet refused to adopt that line of action, then that would count decisively against the conceptual legitimacy of saying that it was *really* his will to attain that end. To proceed in this way at least appears to involve treating the principle as a necessary truth. On the other hand, one might also be inclined to regard the principle as offering a general account of a certain aspect of our psychological processes, as specifying a condition under which, when our will is fixed on a certain object, it will be the case that it is also fixed on a certain other object; to take this view of the principle seems like regarding it as a psychological law and so as contingent. My second problem (Problem B) is, then, this: how (without a blanket rejection of the analytic/ synthetic distinction) are we to account for and, if possible, resolve the ambivalence concerning their status with which we seem to look upon certain principles involving psychological concepts?

To set this problem aside for a moment, the approach

which I am interested in exploring is that of thinking of certain central psychological concepts as *theoretical concepts*; they are *psychological* concepts just because they are the primitive concepts which belong to a certain kind of psychological theory without also belonging to any presupposed theory (such as physiological theory); and a psychological theory is a theory whose function is to provide, in a systematic way, explanations of behaviour which differ from any explanations of behaviour which may be provided by (or may some day be provided by) any presupposed theory (such as physiological theory). To explicate such psychological concepts is to characterize their role in the theory to which they primarily belong, to specify (with this or that degree of detail) the laws or quasi-laws in which they figure, and the manner in which such laws are linked to behaviour. Now to say this much is not to say anything very new; I am sure you have heard this sort of thing before. It is also not to say *very much*; all that has so far been given is a sketch of a programme for the philosophical treatment of psychological concepts, not even the beginnings of a philosophical treatment itself. What is needed is rather more attention to detail than is usually offered by advocates of this approach; we need to pursue such questions as what the special features of a psychological theory are, why such a theory should be needed, what sort of laws or generalities it should contain, and precisely how such laws may be used to explicate familiar psychological terms. I shall be addressing myself to some of these questions in the remainder of this address to you.

But before any more is said, a further problem looms. I can almost hear a murmur to the effect that such an approach to philosophical psychology is doomed from the start. Do we not have *privileged access* to our own beliefs and desires? And, worse still, may it not be true that at least some of our avowals of our beliefs and desires are *incorrigible*? How, then, are such considerations as these to be rendered consistent with an approach which seems to imply that the justifiability of attributing beliefs and desires to people (and maybe animals), *including ourselves*, rests on the utility of the theory to which the concepts of belief and desire belong, in providing desiderated explanations of behaviour? This is my third problem (Problem C).

My fourth problem (D: the *Selection Problem*) is connected with a different and less radical objection to the approach which I have just begun to sketch. Surely, it may be said, it cannot be right to suppose that a conjunction of *all* the laws of a psychological theory in which a psychological concept figures is what should be used to explicate that concept. Even if we are in a position to use some of these laws (which is not certain), we are not, and indeed never shall be, in a position to use *all* of them. Moreover, some particular laws are not going to be suitable. For all we know, some modification of one or other of the following laws[2] might be a psychological law, possibly an underived law:

1. Optimism Law: the more one wants ϕ the more likely one is to believe ϕ .
2. Optimism/Pessimism Law: given condition C_1, the more one wants ϕ, the *more* likely one is to believe ϕ; given condition C_2, the more one wants ϕ, the *less* likely one is to believe ϕ.

These do not seem the right *kind* of laws to be used to explicate wanting and believing. We need some selective principle: what is it?

II. Some General Aspects of the Relation between Psychological Theory and Psychological Concepts

First, a preliminary observation: if we are seeking to explicate psychological concepts by relating them to a

---

[2] Examples by courtesy of Judy Baker.

psychological theory, the theory which we invoke should be one which can be regarded as underlying our ordinary speech and thought about psychological matters, and as such will have to be a part of folk-science. There is no need to suppose that its structure would be of a sort which is appropriate for a *professional* theory, nor even to suppose that it would be a correct or acceptable theory; though I would hope that there would be a way of showing that at least some central parts of it would be interpretable within an acceptable professional theory in such a way as to come out true in that theory, and that indeed this demand might constitute a constraint on the construction of a professional theory. This is perhaps a latter-day version of a defence of common sense in this area.[3]

Let us unrealistically suppose, for the purposes of schematic discussion, that we have a psychological theory which, when set out in formal dress, contains a body of underived laws, the formulation of which incorporates two primitive predicate-constants, J and V; these we want to correspond, respectively, to two psychological terms "judging" and "willing", which in their turn will serve as a regimented base for the explication of such familiar notions as believing and wanting. Let us think of J and V as correlated with, or ranging over, "instantiables", leaving open the question whether these instantiables are sets or properties, or both, or neither. Let us abbreviate the conjunction of these laws by "L", and let us ignore for the moment the obvious fact that any adequate theory along these lines would need to distinguish specific sub-instantiables under J and V, corresponding to the diversity of specific contents which judging and willing may take as modifications (as "intentional objects").

How are we to envisage the terms "judge" and "will" as being introduced? Two closely related alternative ways suggest themselves. First, what I shall call the way of

---

[3] This topic will be touched upon somewhat more fully in Section VIII.

Ramsified naming: 'There is just one *J* and just one *V* such that *L*, and let *J* be called "judging" and V be called "willing".' On this alternative, the uniqueness claim is essential, since "judging" and "willing" are being assigned as names for particular instantiables. The second alternative, which I may call the way of Ramsified definition, can dispense with the uniqueness claim. It will run: '(*a*) *x* judges just in case there is a *J* and there is a *V* such that *L*, and *x* instantiates *J*; (*b*) *x* wills just in case there is a *J* and there is a *V* such that *L*, and *x* instantiates *V*.'

We now have available a possible explanation of the ambivalence we may feel with regard to the status of certain psychological principles, which was the subject of Problem *B*. The difference between the two alternative procedures is relatively subtle, and if we do not distinguish them we may find ourselves under the pull of both. But the first alternative will render certain psychological principles contingent, while the second will render the same principles non-contingent. Let me illustrate by using an even simpler and even less realistic example. Suppose that a psychological law tells us that anyone in state *P* hollers, and that we seek to use this law to introduce the term "pain". On the first alternative, we have: there is just one *P*, such that anyone in state *P* hollers, and let us call *P* "pain". Since on this alternative we are naming the state *P* "pain", if the utilized law is contingent, so will be the principle 'anyone who is in pain hollers.' If we use the second alternative, we shall introduce "pain" as follows: *x* is in pain just in case there is a *P* such that anyone in state *P* hollers and *x* is in state *P*. On this alternative it will be non-contingently true that anyone who is in pain hollers. (For to be in pain is to be in some state which involves hollering.) While this suggestion may account for the ambivalence noted, it does not of course resolve it; to resolve it, one would have to find a reason for preferring one of the alternatives to the other.

In a somewhat devious pursuit of such a reason, let us

enquire further about the character of the postulated psychological instantiables—are they, or could they be, identifiable with physical (physiological) instantiables? One possible position of a sort which has been found attractive by some slightly impetuous physicalists would be to adopt the first alternative (that of Ramsified naming) and to combine it with the thesis that the *J*-instantiable is to be identified with one physiological property and the *V*-instantiable with another such property. This position at least appears to have the feature, to which some might strongly object, of propounding a seemingly philosophical thesis which is at the mercy of possible developments in physiology; and, one might add, the prospects that such developments would be favourable to the thesis do not seem to be all that bright. The adaptiveness of organisms may well be such as to make it very much in the cards that different creatures of the same species may, under different environmental pressures, develop different sub-systems (even different sub-systems at different times) as the physiological underlay of the same set of psychological instantiables, and that a given physiological property may be the correlate in one sub-system of a particular psychological instantiable, while in another it is correlated with a different psychological instantiable, or with none at all. Such a possibility would mean that a physiological property which was, for a particular creature at a particular time, correlated with a particular psychological instantiable would be neither a necessary nor a sufficient condition for that instantiable; it would at best be sufficient (and perhaps also necessary) for the instantiable *within the particular kind of sub-system* prevailing in the creature at the time. The unqualified identification of the property and the instantiable would now be excluded.

Faced with such a difficulty, a physicalist might resort to various manoeuvres. He might seek to identify a particular psychological instantiable with a disjunctive property, each disjoined constituent of which is a property consisting in having a certain physiological property in a certain kind of sub-system; or he might relativize the notion of identity, for the purpose of psycho-physical identification, to types of sub-systems; or he might abandon the pursuit of identification at the level of instantiables, and restrict himself to claiming identities between individual psychological events or states of affairs (e.g. Jones's believing at *t* that *p*) and physiological events or states of affairs (e.g. Jones's brain being in such and such a state at *t*). But none of these shifts has the intuitive appeal of their simplistic forebear. Moreover, each will be open to variants of a familiar kind of objection. For example, Jones's judging at noon that they were out to get him might well be a case of judging something to be true on insufficient evidence; but (to use Berkeley's phrase) it 'sounds harsh' to say that Jones's brain's being in such and such a state at noon is a case of judging something to be true on insufficient evidence. For my part, I would hope that a much-needed general theory of categories would protect me against any thesis which would require me either to license such locutions as the last *or* to resort to a never-ending stream of cries of 'Opaque context!' in order to block them. If the prime purpose of the notion of identity is, as I believe it to be, to license predicate-transfers, one begins to look a little silly if one first champions a particular kind of identification, and then constantly jibs at the predicate-transfers which it seems to allow.

Such considerations as these can, I think, be deployed against the way of Ramsified naming even when it is unaccompanied by a thesis about psycho-physical identities. However unlikely it may be that the future course of physiological research will favour any simple correlations between particular psychological instantiables and particular physiological properties, I do not see that I have any firm guarantee that it will not, that it will never be established that some particular kind of brain state is associated with, say, judging that snow is white. If so, then if I adopt the first alternative with its uniqueness claim, I have no firm guarantee against having to identify my brain's being in some particular state with my judging that snow is white, and so being landed with the embarrassments I have just commented upon. Since I am inclined to think that I do in fact have such a guarantee (although at the moment I cannot lay my hands on it), I am inclined to prefer the second alternative to the first.

As a pendant to the discussion just concluded, let me express two prejudices. First, any psycho-physical identifications which are accepted will have to be accepted on the basis of some known or assumed psycho-physical correlations; and it seems to me that in this area all that philosophical psychology really requires is the supposition that there are such correlations. Whether they do or do not provide a legitimate foundation for *identifications* seems to me to be more a question in the theory of identity than in the philosophy of mind. Second, I am not greatly enamoured of some of the motivations which prompt the advocacy of psycho-physical identifications; I have in mind a concern to exclude such 'queer' or 'mysterious' entities as souls, purely mental events, purely mental properties, and so forth. My taste is for keeping open house for all sorts and conditions of entities, just so long as when they come in they help with the housework. Provided that I can see them at work, and provided that they are not detected in illicit logical behaviour (within which I do not include a certain degree of indeterminacy, not even of numerical indeterminacy), I do not find them queer or mysterious at all. To fangle a new ontological Marxism, *they work therefore they exist*, even though only some, perhaps those who come on the recommendation of some form of transcendental argument, may qualify for the specially favoured status of *entia realissima*. To exclude honest working entities seems to me like metaphysical snobbery, a reluctance to be seen in the company of any but the best objects.

III. *The Form of Psychological "Laws"*

In this section I shall briefly discuss two formal features which I think it might be desirable to attribute to some at least of the laws or quasi-laws of the theory to be used to explicate psychological concepts.

1. Aristotle distinguished between things which are so of necessity and things which are so for the most part, and located in the second category things which are done. More or less conformably with this position, I shall suggest that some or all of the laws which determine psychological concepts are *ceteris paribus* laws, which resemble probability generalizations in that they are defeasible, but differ from them in that *ceteris paribus* laws do not assign weights. I envisage a system which without inconsistency may contain a sequence consisting of a head-law of the form *A's are Z*, and modifying laws of the form *A's which are B are Z'* (where Z' is incompatible with Z), and of the form *A's which are B and C are Z*, and so on. Analogous sequences can be constructed for functional laws; if A, B, and Z are determinables we may have, in the same system:

(a) things which are A to degree α are Z to degree $f^1(\alpha)$
(b) things which are A to degree α and B to degree β are Z to a degree which is the value of $f^2(\beta, f^1(\alpha))$

If we like, we can prefix "*ceteris paribus*" to each such generality, to ensure that "*A's are Z*" is not taken as synonymous with "All *A's are Z.*" For any such system a restriction on *Modus Ponens* is required, since we must not be allowed to infer from *A's are Z* and *x is both A and B* to *x is Z* if *A's which are B are Z'* (where Z' is incompatible with Z) is a law. This restriction will be analogous to the Principle of Total Evidence required for probabilistic systems; a first approximation might run as follows: in applying a law of the system to an individual case for the purpose of detachment, one must select the law with the most specific antecedent which is satisfied by the individual case. Two results of treating psychological laws as *ceteris paribus* laws which will be attractive to me are first that it can no longer be claimed that we do not know any psychological laws because we do not know all the restrictive conditions, and second, that a psychological theory may be included in a larger theory which modifies it; modification does not require emendation.

If a modifying sequence terminates, then its constituent laws can be converted into universal laws; otherwise not. If we hold a strong version of Determinism (roughly, that there is an acceptable theory in which every phenomenon is explained), we might expect the Last Trump to herald a Presidential Address in which the Final Theory is presented, entirely free from *ceteris paribus* laws; but if we accept only a weaker version, with reversed quantifiers (for every phenomenon there is an acceptable theory in which it is explained), the programme for Judgement Day will lose one leading attraction: other items on the agenda, however, may prove sufficiently exciting to compensate for this loss.

2. I suspect that even the latitude given to our prospective psychological folk-theory by allowing it to contain or even consist of *ceteris paribus* laws will not make it folksy enough. There is (or was) in Empirical Psychology a generality called "The Yerkes–Dodson Law"; based on experiments designed to test degrees of learning competence in rats set to run mazes under water, after varying periods of initial constraint, it states (in effect) that, with other factors constant, degrees of learning competence are correlated with degrees of emotional stress by a function whose values form a bell-curve. I have some reluctance towards calling this statement the expression of a law, on the grounds that, since it does not (and could not, given that quantitative expression of degrees of competence and of stress is not available) specify the function or functions in question, it states that *there is* a law of a certain sort

rather than actually state a law. But whether or not the Yerkes–Dodson Law is properly so-called, it is certainly 'law-allusive'; and the feature of being law-allusive is one which I would expect to find in the psychological 'laws' to be used to explicate psychological concepts.

IV. Semi-realistic Procedure for Introducing some Psychological Concepts

I turn now to the task of outlining, in a constructive way, the kind of method by which, in accordance with my programme, particular psychological concepts, and linguistic expressions for them, might be introduced; I shall take into account the need to clarify the routes by which psychological sub-instantiables come to be expressed by the combination of a general psychological verb and a complement which specifies content. My account will be only semi-realistic, since I shall consider the psychological explanation of only a very rudimentary sample of behaviour, and even with respect to that sample a proper explanation would involve apparatus which I omit—for example, apparatus to deal with conceptual representation and with the fact that motivations towards a particular sort of behaviour may be frustrated. But since I am attempting only to illustrate a general method, not to make substantial proposals, these over-simplifications should not matter. I construct my account as if I espoused the first alternative discussed in Section II (the way of Ramsified naming) rather than the second, since that considerably simplifies exposition: a transition to the second alternative can, of course, be quite easily effected.

Let us suppose that a squarrel (a creature something like a squirrel) has some nuts in front of it, and proceeds to gobble them; and that we are interested in the further explanation of this occurrence. Let us call the squarrel "Toby". Our ethological observations of Toby, and of other squarrels, tell us that Toby and other squarrels often gobble nuts in front of them, and also other things besides nuts, and indeed that they are particularly liable to do some gobbling after a relatively prolonged period in which they have done no gobbling at all. On the basis of these observations, and perhaps a range of other observations as well, we decide that certain behaviour of squarrels, including Toby's gobbling nuts in front of him, are suitable subjects for psychological explanation; so we undertake to introduce some theoretical apparatus which can be used to erect an explanatory bridge between Toby's having nuts in front of him, and his gobbling them.

We make the following postulations (if we have not already made them long ago):

1. That the appropriate explanatory laws will refer to three instantiables P, J, and V which (we stipulate) are to be labelled respectively "prehend", "join", and "will".

2. That for any type of creature T there is a class $\hat{N}$ of kinds of thing, which is a class of what (we stipulate) shall be called "necessities for T", and that N (in $\hat{N}$) is a necessity for T just in case N is vital for T, that is, just in case any member of T which suffers a sufficiently prolonged non-intake of N will lose the capacity for all of those operations (including the intake of N), the capacity for which is constitutive of membership of T [in a fuller account this condition would require further explication].

3. That if N is a necessity for T, then *ceteris paribus* a moderately prolonged non-intake of N on the part of a member (x) of T will cause x to instantiate a particular sub-instantiable V_i of "will", x's instantiation of which will (*ceteris paribus*) be quenched by a moderately prolonged intake of N; and (we stipulate) V_i shall be called "will for N" (or, if you like, "willing N").

4. That for any member x (e.g. Toby) of any creature-type T (e.g. squarrels) there is a class $\hat{F}$ of object-types (which, we stipulate, is a class of what shall be called

"object-types familiar to x"); a class $\hat{R}$ of relations (a class of what shall be called "relations familiar to x"), and a class $\hat{A}$ of action-types (a class of what shall be called "action-types in the repertoire of x"), which satisfy the following conditions:

(*a*) that there are two ways (if you like, functions) w_1 and w_2 such that *ceteris paribus* if an instance of an object-type F (familiar to x) is related to x by a relation R (familiar to x), then this causes x to instantiate a sub-instantiable of *prehending* which corresponds in ways w_1 and w_2 to F and R respectively; which sub-instantiable (we stipulate) shall be called "prehending an F as R" [e.g. "prehending nuts as in front"].

(*b*) that *ceteris paribus* if, for some N [e.g. 'squarrel-food'] which is a necessity for x's type, for some A which is in x's repertoire, and for some F and R familiar to x, x has sufficiently frequently, when instantiating *will for* N, performed A upon instances of F which have been related by R to x, and as a result has ceased to instantiate *will* for N: *then* x instantiates a corresponding [corresponding to N, A, F, R] sub-instantiable of *join*ing; which sub-instantiable shall be called "joining N with A and F and R".

We can now formulate an "overall" law (a "PJV Law"), in which we no longer need to restrict N, A, F, and R to members of classes connected in certain ways with a particular creature or type of creature, as follows:

5. *Ceteris paribus*, a creature x which wills N, prehends an F as R, and joins N and A and F and R, performs A. *Finally*, we can introduce "judging" by derivation from "joining"; we stipulate that if x joins N with A and F and R, then we shall speak of x as judging A, *upon-F-in-R, for* N [e.g. judging *gobbling, upon nuts (in) in front, for squarrel-food*].

We now have the desired explanatory bridge.
  (i) Toby has nuts in front of him;
 (ii) Toby is short on squarrel-food (observed or assumed); so
(iii) Toby wills squarrel-food [by postulate 3, connecting will with intake of *N*];
 (iv) Toby prehends nuts as in front [from (i) by postulate 4(*a*), if it is assumed that *nuts* and *in front* are familiar to Toby];
  (v) Toby joins squarrel-food with gobbling and nuts and in front (Toby judges *gobbling, on nuts in front, for squarrel-food*) [by postulate 4(*b*), with the aid of prior observation]; so, by the PJV Law, from (iii), (iv), and (v),
 (vi) Toby gobbles; and, since nuts *are* in front of him, gobbles the nuts in front of him.

I shall end this section by some general remarks about the procedure just sketched.

1. The strategy is relatively simple; we invoke certain *ceteris paribus* laws in order to *introduce* particular psychological sub-instantiables and their specification by reference to content: thus "willing *N*" is introduced as the specific form of willing which is dependent on the intake and deprivation of a necessity *N*, "prehending *F* as *R*" as the variety of prehension which normally results from an *F* being *R* to one, and similarly for "joining". Then we use a further "overall" *ceteris paribus* law to *eliminate* reference to the psychological instantiables and to reach the behaviour which is to be explained. A more developed account would (no doubt) bring in intermediate laws, relating simply to psychological instantiables and not also to features of the common world.

2. The generalities used have at various points the 'law-allusiveness' mentioned in Section III. Every reference to, for example, 'a sufficiently prolonged deprivation', 'a sufficiently frequent performance', or to 'correspondence

in certain ways' in effect implies a demand on some more developed theory actually to produce laws which are here only asserted to be producible.

3. The psychological concepts introduced have been defined only for a very narrow range of complements. Thus, judging has so far been defined only for complements which correspond in a certain way with those involved in the expression of *hypothetical* judgements (judging is, one might say, so far only a species of "if-judging"); and "will" has been defined, so far, only for complements specifying necessities. Attention would have to be given to the provision of procedures for extending the range of these concepts.

4. If the procedure is, in its general character, correct (and I have not even attempted to *show* that it is), the possibility of impact on some familiar philosophical issues is already discernible. To consider only "prehension", which is intended as a prototype for perception:

(*a*) "Prehending F as R" lacks the existential implication that there is an F which is R to the prehender; this condition could be added, but it would be *added*. This might well please friends of sense-data.

(*b*) The fact that reference to physical situations has to be made in the introduction of expressions for specific prehensions might well be very unwelcome to certain phenomenalists.

(*c*) The fact that in the introduction of expressions for specific prehensions a demand is imposed on a further theory to define functions mapping such prehensions on to physical situations might well prove fatal to a sceptic about the material world. How can such a sceptic, who is unsceptical about descriptions of sense-experience, combine the demand implicit in such descriptions with a refusal to assent to the existence of the physical situations which, it seems, the further theory would require in order to be in a position to meet the demand?

V. Creature Construction

I have so far been occupying myself with questions about the structure of the kind of psychological theory which would fulfil the function of bestowing the breath of life on psychological concepts. I shall move now to asking by what methods one might hope to arrive at an acceptable theory of this sort.

One procedure, which I do not in the least despise, would be to take as a body of data our linguistic intuitions concerning what we would or would not be prepared to say when using psychological terms; then, as a first stage, to look for principles (perhaps involving artificially constructed concepts) which would seem to generalize the features of this or that section of our discourse, making adjustments when provisionally accepted principles lead to counter-intuitive or paradoxical results; and, as a second stage, to attempt to systematize the principles which have emerged piecemeal in the first stage, paying attention to the adequacy of a theory so constructed to account for the data conformably with general criteria for the assessment of theories. This would be to operate in two stages approximately corresponding to what the Greeks called the "analytic" (or "dialectical") and the "synthetic" procedures.

I am, for various reasons, not happy to confine myself to these methods. In applying them, many alternative theoretical options may be available, which will often be difficult to hit upon. I would like, if it is possible, to find a procedure which would tell me sooner and louder if I am on the right track, a procedure, indeed, which might in the end tell me that a particular theory is the right one, by some test beyond that of the ease and elegance with which it accommodates the data. I suspect that a dividend of this sort was what Kant expected transcendental arguments to yield, and I would like a basis for the construction of some analogue of transcendental arguments. I am also

influenced by a different consideration. I am much im-
pressed by the fact that arrays of psychological concepts, of
differing degrees of richness, are applicable to creatures of
differing degrees of complexity, with human beings (so far)
at the peak. So I would like a procedure which would do
justice to this kind of continuity, and would not leave me
just pursuing a number of separate psychological theories
for different types of creatures.

The method which I should like to apply is to construct
(in imagination, of course), according to certain principles
of construction, a type of creature, or rather a sequence of
types of creature, to serve as a model (or models) for actual
creatures. My creatures I call *pirots* (which, Russell and
Carnap have told us, are things which karulize elatically).
The general idea is to develop sequentially the psychological theory for different brands of pirot, and to compare
what one thus generates with the psychological concepts
we apply to suitably related actual creatures, and when
inadequacies appear, to go back to the drawing-board to
extend or emend the construction (which of course is
unlikely ever to be more than partial).

The principles of pirot-construction may be thought of
as embodied in what I shall call a genitorial programme,
the main aspects of which I shall now formulate.

1. We place ourselves in the position of a *genitor*, who
is engaged in designing living things (or rather, as I shall
say, *operants*). An operant may, for present purposes, be
taken to be a thing for which there is a certain set of
operations requiring expenditure of energy stored in the
operant, a sufficient frequency of *each* operation in the set
being necessary to maintain the operant in a condition to
perform *any* in the set (i.e. to avoid becoming an ex-
operant). Specific differences within such sets will determine different types of operant. The genitor will *at least*
have to design them with a view to their survival
(continued operancy); for, on certain marginal assumptions which it will be reasonable for us to make but tedious

for me to enumerate, if an operant (x) is not survival-oriented, there is no basis for supposing it to exist at all; since (by the assumption) x has to be produced in some way or other by other operants of the type, x will not exist unless pro-genitors are around to produce it; and if they are to have the staying power (and other endowments) required for x's production, x, being of the same type, must be given the same attributes. So in providing for the individual x, some provision for the continuation of the type is implicit. In order to achieve economy in assumptions, we shall suppose the genitor to be concerned *only* to optimize survival chances.

2. Since the genitor is only a fiction, he is to be supposed only to design, not to create. In order that his designs should be useful to philosophical psychology, he must be supposed to pass his designs on to the engineer (who, being also a fiction, also does not have the power to create): the function of the engineer is to ensure that the designs of the genitor can be realized in an organism which behaves according to pre-psychological laws (e.g. those of physics and physiology). Since the genitor does not know about engineering, and since he does not want to produce futile designs, he had better keep a close eye on the actual world in order to stay within the bounds of the possible.

3. The mode of construction is to be thought of as being relative to some very generally framed "living-condition" concerning the relation of a pirot to its environment; the operations the capacity for which determines the type of the pirot are to be those which, given the posited condition, constitute the minimum which the pirot would require in order to optimize the chances of his remaining in a condition to perform just those operations. Some pirots (plant-like) will not require psychological apparatus in order that their operations should be explicably performed; others will. Within the latter class, an ascending order of psychological types would, I hope, be generated by increasing the degree of demandingness in the determining

condition. I cannot specify, at present, the kind of generality which is to attach to such conditions; but I have in mind such a sequence as operants which do not need to move at all to absorb sources of energy, operants which only have to make posture changes, operants which, because the sources are not constantly abundant, have to locate those sources, and (probably a good deal later in the sequence) operants who are maximally equipped to cope with an indefinite variety of physiologically tolerable environments (i.e., perhaps, rational pirots). Further types (or sub-types) might be generated by varying the degree of effectiveness demanded with respect to a given living-condition.

4. Aristotle regarded types of soul (as I would suppose, of living thing) as forming a "developing series". I interpret that idea as being the supposition that the psychological theory for a given type is an extension of, and includes, the psychological theory of its predecessor-type. The realization of this idea is at least made possible by the assumption that psychological laws may be of a *ceteris paribus* form, and so can be modified without emendation. If this aspect of the programme can be made good, we may hope to safeguard the unity of psychological concepts in their application to animals and to human beings. Though (as Wittgenstein noted) certain animals can only *expect* such items as food, while men can expect a drought next summer, we can (if we wish) regard *the* concept of expectation as being determined not by the laws relating to it which are found in a single psychological theory, but by the sequences of sets of laws relating to it which are found in an ascending succession of psychological theories.

5. Since the genitor is only to install psychological apparatus in so far as it is required for the generation of operations which would promote survival in a posited living-condition, no psychological concept can be instantiated by a pirot without the supposition of behaviour which

manifests it. An explanatory concept has no hold if there is nothing for it to explain. This is why 'inner states must have outward manifestations'.

6. Finally, we may observe that we now have to hand a possible solution of the Selection Problem (D). Only those laws which can be given a genitorial justification (which fall within 'Pure Psychology') will be counted as helping to determine a psychological concept. It is just because one is dubious about providing such a justification for the envisaged "Optimism" laws that one is reluctant to regard either of them as contributing to the definition of believing and wanting.

Kant thought that, in relation to the philosophy of nature, ideas of pure reason could legitimately be given only a regulative employment; somewhat similarly, as far as philosophical psychology is concerned, I think of the genitorial programme (at least in the form just characterized) as being primarily a heuristic device. I would, however, hope to be able to retain a less vivid reformulation of it, in which references to the genitor's purposes would be replaced by references to final causes, or (more positivistically) to survival-utility; this reformulation I would hope to be able to use to cope with such matters as the Selection problem. But (also much as Kant thought with respect to ideas of pure reason) when it comes to ethics the genitorial programme, in its more colourful form, just *may* have a role which is not purely heuristic. The thought that if one were genitor, one would install a certain feature which characteristically leads to certain forms of behaviour might conceivably be a proper step in the *evaluation* of that feature and of the associated behaviour.

Let me be a little more explicit, and a great deal more speculative, about the possible relation to ethics of my programme for philosophical psychology. I shall suppose that the genitorial programme has been realized to the point at which we have designed a class of pirots which, nearly following Locke (*Essay*, II. 27. 8), I might call 'very intelligent rational pirots'. These pirots will be capable of putting themselves in the genitorial position, of asking how, if they were constructing themselves with a view to their own survival, they would execute this task; and if we have done our work aright, their answer will be the same as ours. In virtue of the rational capacities and dispositions which we have given them, and which they would give themselves, each of them will have both the capacity and the desire to raise the further question 'Why go on surviving?'; and (I hope) will be able to justify his continued existence by endorsing (in virtue of the afore-mentioned rational capacities and dispositions) a set of criteria for evaluating and ordering ends, and by applying these criteria both to ends which he may already have, as indirect aids to survival, and to ends which are yet to be selected; such ends, I may say, will not necessarily be restricted to concerns for himself. The justification of the pursuit of some system of ends would, in its turn, provide a justification for his continued existence.

We might, indeed, envisage the contents of a highly general practical manual, which these pirots would be in a position to compile; this manual, though perhaps short, might serve as a basis for more specialized manuals to be composed when the pirots have been diversified by the harsh realities of actual existence. The contents of the initial manual would have various kinds of generality which are connected with familiar discussions of universalizability. The pirots have, so far, been endowed only with the characteristics which belong to the genitorially justified psychological theory; so the manual will have to be formulated in terms of the concepts of that theory, together with the concepts involved in the very general description of living-conditions which have been used to set up that theory; the manual will therefore have *conceptual generality*. There will be no way of singling out a special subclass of addresses, so the injunctions of the manual will have to be addressed, indifferently, to any very intelligent rational pirot, and will thus have *generality of form*. And since the manual can be thought of as being composed by each of the so far indistinguishable pirots, no pirot would include in the manual injunctions prescribing a certain line of conduct in circumstances to which he was not likely to be subject; nor indeed *could* he do so, even if he would. So the circumstances for which conduct is prescribed could be presumed to be such as to be satisfied, from time to time, by any addressee; the manual, then, will have *generality of application*.

Such a manual might, perhaps, without ineptitude be called an IMMANUEL; and the very intelligent rational pirots, each of whom both composes it and from time to time heeds it, might indeed be ourselves (in our better moments, of course).

VI. *Type-Progression in Pirotology: Content-Internalization*

My purpose in this section is to give a little thought to the question 'What are the general principles exemplified, in creature-construction, in progressing from one type of pirot to a higher type? What *kinds* of steps are being made?' The kinds of step with which I shall deal here are those which culminate in a licence to include, within the specification of the content of the psychological state of certain pirots, a range of expressions which would be inappropriate with respect to lower pirots; such expressions include connectives, quantifiers, temporal modifiers, mood-indicators, modal operators, and (importantly) names of psychological states like "judge" and "will"; expressions the availability of which leads to the structural enrichment of specifications of content. In general, these steps will be ones by which items or ideas which have, initially, a legitimate place outside the scope of psychological instantiables (or, if you will, the expressions for which occur legitimately outside the scope of psychological verbs) come to have a legitimate place within the scope of such instantiables: steps by which (one might say) such items or ideas come to be *internalized*.

I am disposed to regard as prototypical the sort of natural disposition which Hume attributes to us, and which is very important to him; namely, the tendency of the mind 'to spread itself upon objects', to project into the world items which, properly (or primitively) considered, are really features of our states of mind. Though there are other examples in his work, the most famous case in which he tries to make use of this tendency to deal with a philosophical issue is his treatment of necessity; the idea of necessary connection is traced (roughly) to an internal impression which attends the passage of the mind from an idea or impression to an associated idea. I am not wholly happy about Hume's characterization of this kind of projection, but what I have to say will bear at least a generic resemblance to what may be found in Hume.

The following kinds of transition seem to me to be characteristic of internalization.

1. References to psychological states (ψ-states) may occur in a variety of linguistic settings which are also appropriate to references to states which have no direct connection with psychology. Like volcanic eruptions, judgings or willings may be assigned both more precise and less precise temporal locations (e.g. last Thursday or next Tuesday, in the future or in the past); sometimes specifications of degree will be appropriate; judging [A] or willing [A] may be assigned a cause or an effect; and references to such ψ-states will be open to logical operations such as negation and disjunction. To suppose that a creature will, in the future, judge [A], or that he either judges [A] or judges [B], is obviously not to attribute to him a judging distinct from judging [A], or from judging [A] and from judging [B]; nevertheless, we can allow a *transition* from these attributions to the attribution of

judgings which are distinct, viz. of "future-judging [A]" (expecting [A]) and of "or-judging [A, B]". Since these are new ψ-states, they will be open to the standard range of linguistic settings for references to ψ-states; a creature may now (or at some time in the future) future-judge [A] (or past-judge [A]). There will be both a semantic difference and a semantic connection (not necessarily the same for every case) between the terminology generated by this kind of transition and the original from which it is generated; while "*x* or-judges [A, B]" will not require the truth of "*x* judges [A] or *x* judges [B]", there will be a connection of meaning between the two forms of expression; if a creature *x* or-judges its potential prey as being [in the tree, in the bush], we may expect *x* to wait in between the tree and the bush, constantly surveying both; or-judging [A, B] will, in short, be typically manifested in behaviour which is appropriate equally to the truth of A and to the truth of B, and which is preparatory for behaviour specially appropriate to the truth of one of the pair, to be evinced when it becomes true either that *x* judges [A] or that *x* judges [B].

This kind of transition, in which an "extrinsic" modifier attachable to ψ-expressions is transformed into (or replaced by) an "intrinsic" modifier (one which is specificatory of a special ψ-state), I shall call *first-stage internalization*.

2. It should be apparent from the foregoing discussion that transitions from a lower type to a higher type of pirot will often involve the addition of diversifications of a ψ-state to be found undiversified in the lower type of pirot; we might proceed, for example, from pirots with a capacity for simple judging to pirots with a capacity for present-judging (the counterpart of the simple judging of their predecessors), and also for future-judging (primitive expecting) and for past-judging (primitive remembering). It may be possible always to represent developmental steps in this way; but I am not yet sure of this. It may be that

sometimes we should attribute to the less-developed pirot two distinct states, say judging and willing; and only to a more developed pirot do we assign a more generic state, say accepting, of which, once it is introduced, we may represent judging and willing as specific forms (judicatively accepting and volitively accepting). But by whatever route we think of ourselves as arriving at it, the representation within a particular level of theory of two or more ψ-states as diversifications of a single generic ψ-state is legitimate, in my view, only if the theory includes laws relating to the generic ψ-state which, so far from being trivially derivable from laws relating to the specific ψ-states, can be used to derive in the theory, as special cases, some but not all generalities which hold for the specific ψ-states. We might, for example, justify the attribution to a pirot of the generic ψ-state of accepting, with judging and willing as diversifications, by pointing to the presence of such a law as the following: *ceteris paribus*, if x or-accepts (in mode m of acceptance) $[A, B]$, and x negatively accepts, in mode m, $[A]$, then x positively accepts, in mode m, $[B]$. From this law we could derive that, *ceteris paribus*, (*a*) if x or-judges $[A, B]$ and negatively judges $[A]$, then x positively judges $[B]$; and (*b*) if x or-wills $[A, B]$ and negatively wills $[A]$, then x positively wills $[B]$. ((*a*) and (*b*) are, of course, psychological counterparts of mood-variant versions of *modus tollendo ponens*.)

3. A further kind of transition is one which I shall label *second-stage internalization*. It involves the replacement of an "intrinsic" modifier, which signifies a differentiating feature of a specific ψ-state, by a corresponding operator within the content-specifications for a less specific ψ-state. If, for example, we have reached by first-stage internalization the ψ-state of future-judging $[A]$, we may proceed by second-stage internalization to the ψ-state of judging [in the future, A]: similarly, we may proceed from judging (judicatively accepting) $[A]$ to accepting [it is the case that A], from willing (volitively accepting) $[A]$ to

accepting [let it be that *A*], and from disjunctively judging (or-judging) [*A*, *B*] to judging [*A* or *B*]. So long as the operator introduced into a content-specification has maximum scope in that specification, the result of second-stage internalization is simply to produce a notational variant: "*x* judges [*A* or *B*]" is semantically equivalent to "*x* disjunctively judges [*A*, *B*]", and if matters rested here, there would be no advance to a new level of theory. To reach a new level of theory, and so to reach ψ-states exemplifiable only by a higher type of pirot, provision must be made for ψ-states with contents in the specification of which the newly introduced operator is embedded within the scope of another operator, as in "*x* judges [if *A* or *B*, *C*]", or in "*x* accepts [if *A*, let it be that *B*]". An obvious consequence of this requirement will be that second-stage internalizations cannot be introduced singly; an embedded operator must occur within the scope of another embeddable operator. The unembedded occurrences of a new operator, for which translation back into the terminology of the previous level of theory is possible, secure continuity between the new level and the old; indeed, I suspect that it is a general condition on the development of one theory from another that there should be cases of "overlap" to ensure continuity, and cases of non-overlap to ensure that a new theory has really been developed.

Two observations remain to be made. First, if we enquire what theoretical purpose is likely to be served by endowing a type of pirot with the capacity for ψ states the specification of which involves embedded operators, one important answer is likely to be that explanation of the ranges of behaviour to be assigned to that type of pirot requires a capacity for a relatively high grade of inference, in which the passage from premisses to conclusion is encompassed, so to speak, within a single thought; the pirot has to be capable, for example, of thinking [since, *A*, *B*, and *C*, then *D*]. This capacity may well require other capacities, e.g. for evaluation, for higher-order states, and so on. There are fascinating and difficult questions about the extent to which a full internalization of one kind of idea or item carries with it full internalization of other kinds of idea or item; but these questions must be deferred to another occasion.

Second, I am sympathetic to two methodological principles relating to internalization. One is that, since principles of parsimony dictate that we introduce no explanatory tool more powerful than is required to do the job, when psychological states which have been generated by first-stage internalization can be seen to be adequate for explanatory purposes, one should not attribute to a pirot the states which would be reached by superimposing second-stage internalization. The other is that, where possible, one should avoid the fully internalized appearance of an idea or item if that appearance has not been preceded, at a lower level of theory, by a first-stage internalization of the idea or item in question; full internalization will be relatively unproblematic if it has come about in accordance with a general pattern for internalization. There are certainly, however, exceptions to the latter principle; one very important kind of internalization, the internalization of psychological instantiables such as judging and willing (as distinct from the internalization of differentiating features of such instantiables) is not easily accommodated within the characterization of procedures for internalization which I have been sketching; and while the two-stage pattern seems appropriate for internalization with respect to tenses, it does not seem appropriate with respect to very specific temporal modifiers like "three weeks from next Tuesday".

Nevertheless, subject to a list of exceptions which I am not in a position to formulate, we might gather up the following provisional list of principles governing internalization:

1. ψ-states generated by internalization should conform to the restrictions propounded in Section VII; that is to say, they should not be assigned to a pirot without (a) the assignment to the pirot of behaviour the presence of which they will be required to explain, and (b) a genitorial justification for the presence of that behaviour in the pirot.

2. If both generic and specific ψ-states are to be recognized by a theory, each such state should figure nontrivially in laws of that theory.

3. Second-stage internalization should be invoked only when first-stage internalization is inadequate for explanatory purposes.

4. Where possible, full internalization should be reached by a standard two-stage progression.

VII. Higher-Order Psychological States

In this section I shall focus on just one of the modes of content-internalization, that in which psychological concepts (or other counterparts in psychological theory) are themselves internalized. I shall give three illustrations of the philosophical potentialities of this mode of internalization, including a suggestion for the solution of my third initial problem (Problem C), that of the accommodation, within my approach, of the phenomena of privileged access and incorrigibility.

1. As I have already remarked, it may be possible in a sufficiently enriched theory to define concepts which have to be treated as primitive in the theory's more impoverished predecessors. Given a type of pirot whose behaviour is sufficiently complex as to require a psychological theory in which psychological concepts, along with such other items as logical connectives and quantifiers, are internalized, it will I think be possible to define a variety of judging, which I shall call "judging*", in terms of willing. I doubt if one

would wish judging* to *replace* the previously distinguished notion of judging; I suspect one would wish them to coexist; one would want one's relatively advanced pirots to be capable not only of the highly rational state of judging* but also of the kind of judging exemplified by lower types, if only in order to attribute to such advanced pirots implicit or unconscious judgings. There may well be more than one option for the definition of judging*; since my purpose is to illustrate a method rather than to make a substantial proposal, I shall select a *relatively* simple way, which may not be the best.

The central ideal is that whereas the proper specification of a (particularized) disposition, say a man's disposition to entertain his brother if his brother comes to town, would be as a disposition to entertain his brother if *he believes that* his brother has come to town (cf. the circularities noted in Section I), no such emendation is required if we speak of a man's *will* to entertain his brother if his brother comes to town. We may expect the man to be disappointed if he discovers that his brother has *actually* come to town without his having had the chance to entertain him, whether or not he was at the time *aware* that his brother was in town. Of course, to put his will into effect on a particular occasion, he will have to judge that his brother is in town, but no reference to such a judgement would be appropriate in the specification of the *content* of his will.

Here, then, is the definition which I suggest. x judges* that p just in case x wills as follows: given any situation in which (i) x wills some end E, (ii) there are two non-empty classes (K_1 and K_2) of action-types such that the performance by x of an action-type belonging to K_1 will realize E just in case p is true, and the performance by x of a member of K_2 will realize E just in case p is false, (iii) there is no third non-empty class (K_3) of action-types, such that the performance by x of an action-type belonging to K_3 will realize E whether p is true or p is false: *then* in such a situation x is to will that he perform some action-type belonging to K_1. Put more informally (and less accurately), x judges* that p just in case x wills that, if he has to choose between a kind of action which will realize some end of his just in case p is true and a kind of action which will realize that end just in case p is false, he should will to adopt some action of the first kind.

2. We might be able to use the idea of higher-order states to account for a kind of indeterminacy which is frequently apparent in our desires. Consider a disgruntled employee who wants more money; and suppose that we embrace the idea (which may *very well* be misguided) of representing his desire in terms of the notion of *wanting that p* (with the aid of quantifiers). To represent him as wanting that he should have some increment or other, or that he should have some increment or other within certain limits, may not do justice to the facts; it might be to attribute to him too *generic* a desire, since he may not be thinking that *any* increment, or *any* increment within certain limits, would do. If, however, we shift from thinking in terms of internal quantification to thinking in terms of external quantification, then we run the risk of attributing to him too *specific* a desire; there may not be any specific increment which is the one he wants; he may just not have yet made up his mind. It is as if we should like to plant our (existential) quantifier in an intermediate position, in the middle of the word 'want'; and that, in a way, is just what we can do. We can suppose him (initially) to be wanting that there be some increment (some increment within certain limits) such that he wants that increment; and then, when under the influence of that want he has engaged in further reflection, or succeeded in eliciting an offer from his employer, he later reaches a position to which external quantification is appropriate; that is, there now is some particular increment such that he wants that increment.

3. I shall now try to bring the idea of higher-order states to bear on Problem C (how to accommodate privileged

access and, maybe, incorrigibility). I shall set out in stages a possible solution along these lines, which will also illustrate the application of aspects of the genitorial programme.

Stage 0. We start with pirots equipped to satisfy unnested judgings and willings (i.e. whose contents do not involve judging or willing).

Stage 1. It would be advantageous to pirots if they could have judgings and willings which relate to the judgings or willings of other pirots; for example, if pirots are sufficiently developed to be able to will their own behaviour in advance (form intentions for future action), it could be advantageous to one pirot to anticipate the behaviour of another by judging that the second pirot *wills* to do *A* (in the future). So we construct a higher type of pirot with this capacity, without however the capacity for *reflexive* states.

Stage 2. It would be advantageous to construct a yet higher type of pirot, with judgings and willings which relate to its own judgings or willings. Such pirots could be equipped to control or regulate their own judgings and willings; they will presumably be already constituted so as to conform to the law that *ceteris paribus* if they will that *p* and judge that not-*p*, then if they can, they make it the case that *p*. To give them some control over their judgings and willings, we need only extend the application of this law to their judgings and willings; we equip them so that *ceteris paribus* if they will that they do not will that *p* and judge that they do will that *p*, then (if they can) they make it the case that they do *not* will that *p* (and we somehow ensure that sometimes they *can* do this). [It may be that the installation of this kind of control would go hand in hand with the installation of the capacity for evaluation; but I need not concern myself with this now.]

Stage 3. We shall not want these pirots to depend, in

reaching their second-order judgements about themselves, on the observation of manifestational behaviour; indeed, if self-control which involves suppressing the willing that p is what the genitor is aiming at, behaviour which manifests a pirot's judging that it wills that p may be part of what he hopes to prevent. So the genitor makes these pirots subject to the law that *ceteris paribus* if a pirot judges (wills) that p, then it judges that it judges (wills) that p. To build in this feature *is* to build in privileged access to judgings and willings.

To minimize the waste of effort which would be involved in trying to suppress a willing which a pirot mistakenly judges itself to have, the genitor may also build in conformity to the converse law, that *ceteris paribus* if a pirot judges that it judges (wills) that p, then it judges (wills) that p. Both of these laws however are only *ceteris paribus* laws; and there will be room for counter-examples; in self-deception, for example, either law may not hold (we may get a judgement that one wills that p without the willing that p, and we may get willing that p without judging that one wills that p—indeed, with judging that one does *not* will that p).

Stage 4. Let me abbreviate "x judges that x judges that p" by "x judges^2 that p", and "x judges that x judges that x judges that p" by "x judges^3 that p". Let us suppose that we make the not implausible assumption that there will be no way of finding *non-linguistic* manifestational behaviour which *distinguishes* judging^3 that p from judging^2 that p. There will now be two options: we may suppose that "judge^3 that p" is an inadmissible locution, which one has no basis for applying; or we may suppose that "x judges^3 that p" and "x judges^2 that p" are manifestationally equivalent, just because there can be no *distinguishing* behavioural manifestation.

The second option is preferable, if (*a*) we want to allow for the construction of a (possibly later) type, a *talking* pirot, which can express that it judges^2 that *p*; and (*b*) to maintain as a general (though probably derivative) law that *ceteris paribus* if *x* expresses that φ then *x* judges that φ. The substitution of "*x* judges^2 that *p*" for " φ" will force the admissibility of "*x* judges^3 that *p*". So we shall have to adopt as a law that *x* judges^3 that *p* iff *x* judges^2 that *p*. Exactly parallel reasoning will force the adoption of the law that *x* judges^4 that *p* if *x* judges^2 that *p*.

If we now define "*x* believes that *p*" as "*x* judges^2 that *p*", we get the result that *x* believes that *p* iff *x* believes that *x* believes that *p*. We get the result, that is to say, that *beliefs* are (in this sense) *incorrigible*, whereas first-order *judgings* are only matters for privileged access.

VIII. *Are Psychological Concepts Eliminable?*

I have tried to shed a little light on the question 'How are psychological concepts related to psychological theory and to psychological explanation?'; I have not, so far, said anything about a question which has considerably vexed some of my friends as well as myself. Someone (let us call him the eliminator) might say: 'You explicitly subscribe to the idea of thinking of psychological concepts as explicable in terms of their roles in psychological laws, that is to say, in terms of their potentialities for the explanation of behaviour. You also subscribe to the idea that, where there is a psychological explanation of a particular behaviour, there is also a physiological explanation; with respect to pirots, it is supposedly the business of the engineer to make psychological states effective by ensuring that this condition holds. You must, however, admit that the explanations of behaviour, drawn from pirot-physiology, which are accessible to the engineer are, from a theoretical point of view, greatly superior to those accessible to the genitor; the former are, for example, drawn from a more comprehensive theory, and from one which yields, or when fully developed will yield, even in the area of behaviour, more numerous and more precise predictions. So since attributions of psychological states owe any claim to truth they may have to their potentialities for the explanation of behaviour, and since these potentialities are inferior to the potentialities of physiological states, Occam's Razor will dictate that attributions of psychological states, to actual creatures no less than to pirots, should be rejected *en bloc* as lacking truth (even though, from ignorance or to avoid excessive labour, we might in fact continue to utter them). We have indeed come face to face with the last gasp of Primitive Animism, namely the attempted perpetuation of the myth that animals are animate.'

The eliminator should receive fuller attention than I can give him on this occasion, but I will provide an interim response to him, in the course of which I shall hope to redeem the promise, made in Section II, to pursue a little further the idea that the common-sense theory which underlines our psychological concepts can be shown to be at least in some respects true.

First, the eliminator's position should, in my view, be seen as a particular case of canonical scepticism, and should, therefore, be met in accordance with general principles for the treatment of sceptical problems. It is necessary, but it is also insufficient, to produce a cogent argument for the falsity of his conclusion; if we confine ourselves to this kind of argumentation we shall find ourselves confronted by the post-eliminator, who says to us 'Certainly the steps in your refutation of the eliminator are validly made; but so are the steps in his argument. A correct view of the matter is that from a set of principles in which psychological concepts occur crucially, and through which those concepts are delineated, it follows both that the eliminator is right and that he is wrong; so much the worse, then, for the set of principles and for the concepts;

they should be rejected as incoherent.' A satisfactory rebuttal of the eliminator's position must, therefore, undermine his argument as well as overturn his conclusion.

In pursuit of the first of these objectives, let me remark that, to my mind, to explain a phenomenon (or sequence of phenomena) P is typically to explain P *qua* exemplifying some particular feature or characteristic; and so one fact or system may explain P *qua* exemplifying characteristic C_1 while another fact or system explains P *qua* exemplifying C_2. In application to the present case, it is quite possible that one system, the physiology of the future, should explain the things we do considered as sequences of *physical movements*, while another system, psychological theory, explains the things we do considered as instances of sorts of *behaviour*. We may, at this point, distinguish two possible principles concerning the acceptability of systems of explanation:

1. If system S_1 is theoretically more adequate, for the explanation of a class of phenomena $\hat{P}$ will respect to a class of characteristics $\hat{C}$, than is system S_2 for the explanation of $\hat{P}$ with respect to $\hat{C}$, then (other things being equal) S_1 is to be accepted and S_2 is to be rejected.

I have no quarrel with this principle.

2. If system S_1 is theoretically more adequate, for the explanation of $\hat{P}$ with respect to $\hat{C}_1$, than is system S_2 for the explanation of $\hat{P}$ with respect to $\hat{C}_2$ [a different class of characteristics], then (other things being equal) S_1 is to be accepted and S_2 is to be rejected.

The latter principle seems to me to lack plausibility; in general, if we want to be able to explain $\hat{P}$ *qua* $\hat{C}_2$ (e.g. as behaviour), our interest in such explanation should not be abandoned merely because the kind of explanation available with respect to some other class of characteristics is theoretically superior to the kind available with respect to $\hat{C}_2$. The eliminator, however, will argue that, in the present case, what we have is really a special case of the application of Principle 1; for since any C_2 (in $\hat{C}_2$) which is exemplified on a given occasion has to be "realized" on that occasion in some C_1 (some sequence of physical movements), for which there is a physiological explanation, the physiological explanation of the presence of C_1 on that occasion is *ipso facto* an explanation of the presence of C_2 (the behavioural feature) on that occasion, and so should be regarded as displacing any psychological explanation of the presence of C_2.

To maintain this position, the eliminator must be prepared to hold that if a behavioural feature is, on an occasion, "realized" in a given type of physical movement-sequence, then that type of movement-sequence is, in itself, a *sufficient condition* for the presence of the behavioural feature; only so can he claim that the full power and prestige of physiological explanation is transmitted from movements to behaviour, thereby ousting psychological explanation. But it is very dubious whether particular movement-sequences are, in general, sufficient conditions for behavioural features, especially with respect to those behavioural features the discrimination of which is most important for the conduct of life. Whether a man with a club is merely advancing towards me or advancing *upon* me may well depend on a condition distinct from the character of his movements, indeed (it would be natural to suppose) upon a *psychological* condition. It might of course be claimed that any such psychological condition would, in principle, be re-expressible in psychological terms, but this claim cannot be made by one who seeks not the reduction of psychological concepts but their rejection: if psychological states are not to be reduced to physiological states, the proceeds of such reduction cannot be used to bridge gaps between movements and behaviour. The truth seems to be that the language of behavioural description is part and parcel of the system to which psychological explanation belongs, and cannot be prised off therefrom. Nor can the eliminator choose to be hanged for a sheep rather than for a mere lamb, by opting to jettison behavioural description along with psychological concepts; he himself will need behavioural terms like "describe" and "report" in order to formulate his non-recommendations (or predictions); and, perhaps more importantly, if there is (or is to be) strictly speaking no such thing as the discrimination of behaviour, then there are (or are to be) no such things as ways of staying alive, either to describe or to adopt.

Furthermore, even if the eliminator were to succeed in bringing psychological concepts beneath the baleful glare of Principle 1, he would only have established that *other things being equal* psychological concepts and psychological explanation are to be rejected. But other things are manifestly not equal, in ways which he has not taken into account. It is one thing to suggest, as I have suggested, that a proper philosophical understanding of ascriptions of psychological concepts is a matter of understanding the roles of such concepts in a psychological theory which explains behaviour; it is quite another thing to suppose that creatures to whom such a theory applies will (or should) be interested in the ascription of psychological states only because of their interest in having a satisfactory system for the explanation of behaviour. The psychological theory which I envisage would be deficient as a theory to explain behaviour if it did not contain provision for interests in the ascription of psychological states otherwise than as tools for explaining and predicting behaviour, interests (for example) on the part of one creature to be able to ascribe these rather than those psychological states to another creature because of a concern for the other creature. Within such a theory it should be possible to derive strong motivations on the part of the creatures subject to the theory against the abandonment of the central concepts of the theory (and so of the theory itself), motivations which the creatures would (or should) regard as justified.[2] Indeed, only from within the framework of such a theory, I think, can matters of evaluation, and so of the evaluation of modes of explanation, be raised at all. If I conjecture aright, then, the entrenched system contains the materials needed to justify its own entrenchment; whereas no rival system contains a basis for the justification of anything at all.

We must be ever watchful against the devil of scientism, who would lead us into myopic over-concentration on the nature and importance of knowledge, and of scientific knowledge in particular; the devil who is even so audacious as to tempt us to call in question the very system of ideas required to make intelligible the idea of calling in question anything at all; and who would even prompt us, in effect, to suggest that, since we do not really think but only think that we think, we had better change our minds without undue delay.[5]

---

[4] Let me illustrate with a little fable. The very eminent and very dedicated neurophysiologist speaks to his wife. "My (for at least a little while longer) dear," he says, "I have long thought of myself as an acute and well-informed interpreter of your actions and behaviour. I think I have been able to identify nearly every thought that has made you smile and nearly every desire that has moved you to act. My researches, however, have made such progress that I shall no longer need to understand you in this way. Instead I shall be in a position, with the aid of instruments which I shall attach to you, to assign to each bodily movement which you make in acting a specific antecedent condition in your cortex. No longer shall I need to concern myself with your so-called thoughts and feelings. In the meantime, perhaps you would have dinner with me tonight. I trust that you will not resist if I bring along some apparatus to help me to determine, as quickly as possible, the physiological idiosyncrasies which obtain in your system."

I have a feeling that the lady might refuse the proffered invitation.

[5] I am indebted to George Myro for the tenor of this remark, as well as for valuable help with the substance of this section.

Index